CW00493618

The 'Bullet' at the Town Hall
Australia Edition

Haydn Thomas

Resarton Books

Published by Resarton Books

132 Great Ancoats Street,
Manchester,
M4 6DE,
Britain.

www.resartonbooks.com

First edition, 2023, paperback
Sixth edition - Australia edition - 2024

ISBN 9781738503889

Copies of the book have been sent to the
relevant legal deposit libraries

Contents

Preface

This book, and "The Cathays Files 25", contains details of numerous criminal and corrupt activities arranged by a high level british government official. Most of them occurred in Britain. When one of his activities started to get out the british government, in 1980, planted false evidence into the situation to keep it covered up.

Some years later, in 1987, the police (british) confirmed (in writing) that they had forged documents that had been made and used by staff in a british university. This was one of the activities arranged by the high level official.

The police knew who used the forged documents (two people), and they probably knew who made them.

A prosecution should of course be started. But a prosecution was not started and the british government imposed censorship on the situation (without an explanation).

A few of the activities arranged by the high level official took place in Australia.

The british government's censorship of this affair has stayed in place up to the publication date of this book. We believe that the end of the censorship is imminent. When it ends they will have to give an explanation for blocking a prosecution in 1987 and placing censorship on the affair. Question 26 in TCF25, seventh edition (page 53), is addressed to the british Prime Minister (Rishi Sunak). I quote the question here for ease of reference.

To the Prime Minister:

(i) Why was a prosecution not started in 1987 when the police had said they had forged documents?

(ii) Why did the government censor this affair (from the 1980s to the date of publication of this book)?

Notes

After the first two chapters in this book (the Preface and GX1) the chapters are given to you in chronological order, until ==== as shown in the Contents. After that the chapters enlarge on various subjects detailed in the earlier chapters and in The Cathays Files 25.

Bear in mind that it was 1975 when I first became aware of the corrupt activities of Group X (Gx1). And that it was the end of 1977, when I started to investigate (look closer at) a number of odd occurrences that had taken place in earlier years (before 1975).

In the years that followed 1977 I gradually obtained a lot more information that showed that Gx1 had, since 1945, been using his high level government position to hit me and my family.

When I say "hit", I mean any act that a person deliberately and covertly does that is intended to adversely affect someone. Examples of adverse effects are to put someone out of a job, or arrange to get him physically hit.

In this book TCF25 means "The Cathays Files 25", 7th edition. TCF6 and TCF9 means the 6th and 9th editions of TCF.

Gx1

In the past I have referred to the high level government official in the Cardiff city hall who covertly tried to kill me (etc) as Group X member number 1, or Group X 1. In "The Cathays Files 25" I referred to him as Gx1. In this book I will continue to refer to him as Gx1.

He married one of my father's sisters in the early 1930s. In the WWII years he was a policeman in Cardiff. Soon after the war finished he went into a job in the Cardiff city hall (as an undercover policeman, in the security services). It is apparent that he was told to keep down ordinary british workers, because they were considered to be commies or potential commies. This coincided with the start of the cold war in 1946.

Note: I use the word commies instead of the word communists.

The Knife in the Trunk

My parents were born in Cardiff and in 1934 they got married in the city. My father was an expert tradesman in the building industry and, with his father, had worked on the construction of the Cardiff museum. In 1935 my parents moved to Nottingham because my father had been offered a good job there. In 1940 they moved back to Cardiff because WWII had started and my father, thinking he would have to join the army, decided that my mother (and young son) would be safer close to her parents in Cardiff.

In 1943/4 my father, in the army, was sent to India. One day, it was probably 1945, he was told to deliver a parcel to a place some distance away from where he was based. He was to take the train and get a train back the same day. However after he delivered the parcel he found that there was no same day return train. He slept the night in a disused railway carriage, and returned the next day.

Some days later my father had malaria. He had obviously picked it up when sleeping rough in the railway carriage (no anti-mosquito netting). He was in a hospital bed for some weeks, close to death, but he came through it okay.

In 1946, with the war having finished, my father returned to Cardiff. A month or two later a metal trunk arrived, he had packed it and posted it when in India. The trunk had been got at, some of what he had put in it had been stolen (presents). However one of the things he had bought, a curved indian dagger in a sheath, was still in it. This is referred to, later in this book, as 'the knife in the trunk'.

My mother was an attractive female. And it's obvious that Gx1 considered this to be the case, as illustrated by some covert 'signs' he gave out years later and a plan he devised in the 1950s to murder my father, by 'natural causes'. With my father dead his wife would be 'available'.

It appears to be very likely that Gx1 used his position (a policeman in Cardiff) to get my father sent on the non-day return train journey, hoping that a night sleeping rough would result in his death by malaria. But the death did not happen and so he arranged, some months later, for the indian dagger to be highlighted, i.e. the presents were stolen from the trunk but the dagger was left in place, to 'say' that the knife was going in to my father at a later date.

I think there were two Gx1 motives in place at this mid 1940s time. One, as I have said, was the desire to make my father's wife available. And the second was the anti-worker, anti-commie, directives that were starting to get fed, by the people that ran this country, into the officials network.

My father was quite obviously a worker, meaning a manual worker, and manual workers were considered (by crude thinkers) to be commies. So Gx1 (who was part of the "officials network") had the idea that by quietly killing my father in 1945 he would be, as well as making his wife 'available', doing a good job for his employers (killing a commie).

My Brother is Poisoned Before
a Welsh Boys Trial

Let's look at my brother's astonishing school athletics day again. It was 1951. The school presented him with the Victor Ludorum medal for being the best athlete in the school (the school I went to didn't have that). This happened in what was presumably his fourth of five years in the school (age 11 to 16). I say this because Gx1 'knifed' him in his fifth year, and this included using his covert influence to get him out of the school before his end of fifth year examinations started ('O' levels). Which means he was not at his fifth year athletics day (which takes place after the examinations).

His school was for pupils aged 11 to 18 (most left school at the age of 16). Presumably the school only presented the one Victor Ludorum medal. Which means that at the age of 15 my brother was a better athlete than the pupils who were aged 16 to 18!

Then three months later he played rugby for Cardiff Boys.

He had also learnt to play the saxophone, and that includes reading music and I believe he played in a dance band a few times. My parents had bought him a saxophone when he was about 12.

His progress in his school studies was excellent. All this adds up to say that my brother was an exceptional individual. And this is why Gx1 (a government policing official, acting on the Cold War stop commies/workers policy that the government had put in place in 1946) moved in, used his covert influence, to put down, stop, my brother's progress, i.e. 'commies' were not to be allowed to get on in our society, and my father, being a manual worker, was, in the mind of Gx1, a commie, and that meant his exceptional son was to be kept down because he was also a commie.

As well as using his covert influence to get my brother out of school before the examinations took place (to ensure he did not get excellent exam results) he also got a hit man to poison my brother days before he was due to play in a trial game for the Wales Boys rugby team (he didn't play in the trial because he was ill, hence he didn't play for Wales Boys). He also stopped my brother's sax playing.

Gx1 preceded these vile 'arrangements' by getting a hit man to break my brother's nose at night when asleep and chloroformed. The purpose of the broken nose was to create one of his 'signs'. The sign said that my brother was going to be 'knifed'. A nose is a trunk, which connected to the 1946 knife in the trunk. At the time it was assumed that my brother had broken his nose during a game of rugby the previous day and hadn't noticed it.

A few years later Gx1 arranged, via conscription, to have my brother shipped out, permanently (to Australia). Gx1 had done his job, he had stopped a very bright 'commie' proceeding, doing well, in british society.

The Mortgage Murder Plan

In 1956 my father obtained a mortgage on a house in Cardiff and we moved into it. The loan was from Cardiff corporation. These days the word council is usually used instead of corporation. It had been arranged by Gx1 who worked in the council offices. It was a fifteen year mortgage (my father had seventeen years of working life left before he reached the retirement age of sixty five).

The house, specially selected by Gx1, was in Malefant Street. In his mind Malefant was elephant, and elephant of course gives trunk. The 'knife in the trunk' would be going into my father when he was living at the house.

The Gx1 plan was to murder my father at the end of the mortgage. At which point a fully paid for house would be transferred into the name of his wife. In other words she would then be 'available' and she would have a lot of money to her name.

The Diamond Hit

This took place on Heath park in Cardiff in May 1960. I was in my first year at my 11-15 school.

The hit was the first of many Gx1 hits that were aimed at ensuring that I did not play in top level rugby (in school, then years later in club rugby).

In the rugby season that had just finished my physical education teacher was very impressed by my rugby and he had plans for me (Cardiff Boys etc). In my end of academic year school report, it was stated that in rugby I was "outstanding".

Gx1, in a high level government job, also had plans, they were to kill my father when he had finished paying his mortgage, and ship me, one way, to Australia. For him, significant success in my rugby, could cause problems for his plans. So he was out to keep down my rugby.

A mid-week game of baseball organised by our physical education teacher, was being played on Heath park and I was participating. Gx1, using covert methods, made me look hopeless, the intention being to start to destroy the big plans for my rugby that the teacher had for me. Details in TCF25, see the section that starts on page 175.

Gx1, years later, used the word diamond to label this hit (a baseball game is played on a diamond).

The Cap over the Cemetery Wall

Gx1, when he arranged covert hit activities, often attached 'signs' to them. In May/June 1960 he arranged the following, it was one of his signs.

I was with a couple of lads on the pavement outside a cemetery that was near our school. One of our caps went over the cemetery wall.

The sign said, 'your playing for the welsh boys is dead', i.e. the Wales Boys cap, which a schoolboy received when he played for Wales, was in a cemetery, 'dead'. Details on this 'dead' cap sign are in TCF25, page 194/5. Also see the chapter "Gx1 Breaks Mr Rowlands Leg" later in this book.

In the next three years Gx1 made sure that my schoolboy rugby went nowhere.

The Sheath Knife

This took place in 1960/61, some months after I experienced the diamond hit on Heath park.

I was in the scouts and Gx1, using his contacts, got my mother to buy a sheath knife for me. It was a large knife and I didn't use it, I didn't even put it on my belt when in scouts uniform. Soon after I lost interest in the scouts and stopped going.

The knife was a Gx1 sign. It said two things:

(i) the knife had been put into me at the diamond hit.

(ii) the knife was going in again, into my father this time, some years on from here, at the new hospital that was planned for Heath park. For Gx1 sheath knife meant Heath knife.

Gx1 Breaks My Brother's Leg

My brother continued to play rugby when he moved to Australia. It was 1960 or '61 when he broke his leg in a rugby game. When this happened it placed a permanent stop on his rugby. He had played for South Australia and he was expected to be selected for the Australia team.

I have no doubt in saying that this was arranged by Gx1. When the expectation that my brother would be in the Australia team appeared the news was forwarded to Gx1 (who got him shipped out in the first place). Gx1 decided, for some reason, that it was not to be allowed to happen. He got the hit carried out using the method he used for Mr HC, see later (laser research was in it's early days but there was enough knowledge around to realise what it could do).

In 1965 Gx1 gave a 'sign' that said that he broke my brother's leg. I will tell you about it.

In 1958 when my brother returned to Australia he travelled by ship. In a letter to us he said that Rolf Harris, an entertainer, was on the ship. This news reached Gx1, my mother often met his wife (my father's sister). In 1965 Rolf Harris produced a song called, "Jake the Peg". This was the Gx1 'sign', it said that he, Gx1, had broken my brother's leg.

How did this 'sign' say that Gx1 had broken my brother's leg? Gx1 had a christian name and two middle names. The initials being PTJ. Well Jake the Peg gives JTP. Jake, the name of the man in the song, said he had an extra leg, the peg being the extra leg, a crutch in other words. When does a man need a crutch? When he has broken (or seriously injured) a leg. Gx1 was covertly saying in this Rolf Harris song that he was the crutch man, the man who arranged to have my brother's leg broken. Details are in TCF25, on pages 213/4.

Here is another Gx1 'sign'. He arranged to have this given to me around 1965. It was a trick. The idea was to make a banana appear as if it had sliced itself. Push a needle into a banana but not right through it. Then swing the needle to the left and the right whilst it is in the banana. Take the needle out and give the banana to someone who is then surprised to find that he has a banana that somehow has sliced itself (it fell apart when he peeled it).

For Gx1 this "trick" was another 'sign' that said he broke my brother's leg. There is three a's in banana, giving Australia with it's three a's. The laser beam done the job of the needle.

A Ship Out 'Sign'

This took place in June 1963 when I was in school aged fifteen.

Some of the pupils in my year were entered for the Duke of Edinburgh's medal award scheme and I was one of them. The bronze medal was the first one to get. To obtain the medal it was necessary to do a couple of small activities that lasted a few hours and then to finish by going on a fifteen mile walk with another pupil and camp out overnight.

The walk was from the school along the A48 to a place fifteen miles west of Cardiff. The lad who did the walk with me lived in Australia Road (which was near the school).

We carried the tent I had (my parents had bought it for my brother in the 1950s) and camped out overnight in a field. In the morning the father of the lad I was with arrived in his car to take us back to Cardiff.

This was Gx1 with a very obvious 'sign'. It was Australia Road for me. I was, in the coming years, on a long walk to Australia.

Gx1, knowing about the scheme, had told my headmaster to put me on it and get a pupil who lived in Australia Road to go with me on the walk.

Gx1 had shipped my brother to Australia in the 1950s and arranged for him to stay there, settle down there. He now planned to ship me there, to live permanently. The ship out date being when my brother and his wife had established themselves in accommodation that was suitable for my arrival (I would stay with him).

In the coming years Gx1 used his position to ensure that I got nowhere, in significant terms, in this country, so as to keep me free from ties for when the ship out date arrived. Being "free from ties" would make it easier for him to ship me out.

To get what he wanted, to ensure his plans stayed on track, he arranged many hits. A "hit" is any act, covertly arranged, that is intended to adversely affect someone.

He often attached a 'sign' to a hit. The 'signs' were in most cases given out in advance of the hit. In other words the 'signs' stated, in covert group x language, what was going to happen. It could be that this was his own way of doing things but it is more likely that he was trained (as a covert policeman) into doing this.

Another Ship Out 'Sign'

I left school at the end of June 1963. Then for the 1963/64 academic year I was on a full time one year course at Llandaff Technical College in Cardiff (where I did 'O' levels). In the summer of 1964 I went to a few job interviews.

One of the interviews I went to was with a company called Firth Cleveland Fastenings. It was located eight miles north of Cardiff.

This was Gx1 with another one of his 'signs'. He somehow got me to apply for the job. The 'sign' said, 'it's leve land for you' (Cleveland). He was again saying he was going to ship me to Australia, one way, in a few years time (to join my brother).

I didn't get the job.

Gx1 arranged a very odd occurrence at this interview. He didn't have to, I mean my just being there gave his 'leve land' 'sign'. He presumably wanted to highlight the 'sign'. If you want to see the details look at the section that starts on page 217 in TCF25.

Gx1 Breaks Mr Rowlands' Leg

When Gx1 got the cap thrown over the cemetery wall in 1960 he knew that in the coming school years he was going to make sure that the physical education teachers plans for me, that I would play for Cardiff Boys and then Wales Boys, did not take place.

In the next six years Gx1 gave two signs that connected to the cap into the cemetery sign. I will tell you about them here.

In the summer of 1964, aged sixteen, I left my full time education and two months later started work. At about this time I decided, with a mate of mine, to start going to Cardiff rugby club games. And this became a regular occurrence, every home game we were there.

When the international games arrived, about February 1965, we went to the Wales v Scotland game at Murrayfield. We travelled by train that left Cardiff on Friday evening for a twelve hour journey. We done our best to get to sleep on the conventional, daytime, seating.

I remember the game for one reason. The Wales scrum half was Clive Rowlands. Every time he got the ball, from a lineout or scrum, he put in an 'up and under' (kicked the ball high and followed up underneath). Perhaps it wasn't "every time" but it seemed like that. When he did it my thoughts were, 'not again - give it out'.

This was a Gx1 sign. He arranged, before the game started, for Clive to be told that every time he got the ball he was to put in an up and under.

The other sign occurred in December 1966. I was

with my rugby mate, DC, watching Cardiff rugby club play on the Arms Park when Keith Rowlands, one of the Cardiff forwards, was carried off on a stretcher. Later we were told by the local press that he had broken a leg. Gx1 did it.

In this hit Gx1 used the same method he used at other times. Keith's leg was weakened, using a laser beam, by a Gx1 hit man during the night before the game when he was asleep and chloroformed/doped. It then broke in the rigours of the game.

Now I will explain why I say that these Clive Rowlands and Keith Rowlands occurrences were covert Gx1 signs.

In 1960, when Gx1 created the dead cap sign, to 'say' my getting a welsh schoolboys rugby cap was 'dead', he had one of my teachers nearby watching, his name was Mr Rowlands (I saw him after the cap went over the cemetery). He reported me to the headmaster and I got caned for it. This cap into the cemetery was part of Gx1's dirty me activities to keep my schoolboy rugby down. One reason for his doing this was that he had a plan to ship me, one way, to Australia in the coming years to join my brother who had got married there and stayed there. Significant success for me in rugby could block the plan.

In the 1965 sign we have Rowlands and 'up and under'. This Gx1 sign said that it was 'up' in a plane for me, 'and under' to Australia. He was pointing out that he had said that my rugby was dead in 1960 but that I could play the game in Australia (perhaps without being hit/restricted).

As for the 1966 sign. Well it could be that Gx1 was repeating that the cap into the cemetery meant my rugby on the Arms Park was dead (where the Cardiff/Wales Boys played). A broken leg for a player means his rugby is dead (no more rugby).

To say that the Clive Rowlands and Keith Rowlands occurrences were not connected to Gx1 is a bit too much for me to take. Three Rowlands right in front of me! As far as I am concerned they are three pieces in the jigsaw puzzle that illustrates the activities of Gx1 because they are an exact fit.

Gx1 was not a rugby man, but he no doubt read the local press because he was part of the governing structure in the Cardiff area. From this he saw the two Rowlands on the sports pages and decided to use them to highlight his cap into the cemetery sign.

The First Gx1 Attempt to Murder Me

In September 1964 I started work as a trainee draughtsman. The job came with one day a week off to attend a college (I also went there two evenings a week).

In 1967 the company I worked for, Associated Electrical Industries, and the college I was going to, Llandaff Technical College, decided that they they were going to get me on to a full time university course (a degree) in September 1968. I knew nothing about this. It was years later when this became apparent to me.

Gx1, in on things, was told about the AEI/Llandaff plan and he did not like it one bit. To start with I was, in his warped mind, a commie, and so should not go to university. But there was more than that. If I went to university it would cause problems for two plans he had. The plan to ship me out of the country (one way), and the plan to murder my father (by 'natural causes'), which was due to take place a few years on from here (when the mortgage was finished).

Gx1 decided that the solution to this awkward situation was to kill me (by 'accident'). With me dead I would not go to university and his plan to murder my father would stay on track. And in September 1967 the attempt to kill me was made. I say "attempt" because it did not succeed. I came through it, unharmed, suspecting nothing.

In the months that followed Gx1 thought up a second plan to kill me. It was to take place in Jersey, a place he knew well.

The 'Hearse' Wristwatch

The first sign that Gx1 gave out for this second plan to kill me was at the end of my AEI job in May 1968. The sign connected me to Jersey, and Summers, a funeral home in Cardiff. I was going to be dead in Jersey.

A second sign he built into his Jersey murder plan was a Seiko watch that he arranged for me to buy three weeks before the kill attempt was to take place (he got me interested in it and with a low price I bought it).

The watch had a small drawing of a sea horse on it's face. In his covert group x language horse was hearse, and sea was where the death was going to take place, i.e. it was going to be death by drowning (the underwater dive, the BD hit, which is detailed in TCF25, pages 86/7). He would have to get me to Jersey and go on a dive but this was no problem for him, being in an 'influential' official position.

This second attempt to kill me, at the end of August 1968, was also a failure. And, because no one had openly attempted to kill me, I again suspected nothing.

I will give you more on this Gx1 Seiko-hearse sign. He had a small dog in the 1960s that he called Sukoo (that's how I spelt it when I first put the word in print).

Sometime after late 1977 (when I started looking closely at occurrences that had taken place before I went to university in 1974) I connected Sukoo and Seiko. I realised that the very odd 1968 Jersey dive had been a Gx1 attempt to kill me. Seiko, with it's sea 'hearse', and the very similar Sukoo, his dog, indicated that he had arranged the dive. The two words were one of his 'connection signs', i.e. I had realised that he sometimes attached covert signs to his activities.

It's now 2023, and I have recently seen on the internet that "Suco Suco" was a popular song in 1961, and it was, it seems, used as a theme tune for a tv series called "Top Secret" that ran for a year or so at that time. It was about british secret agent work. I was aged twelve then and I sometimes watched tv, so I suppose I saw bits of it, but it didn't interest me. Gx1, being a secret agent, in MI5, no doubt watched it and, a few years later, took the word Suco from it, i.e. it gave him his dog's name, which he probably spelt the same way, Suco.

It could be that, having decided that drowning was the way to kill me, he changed the name of his dog from whatever it was to Suco to form his Seiko/Suco, 'I drowned you', sign.

He presumably got a watchmaker to place a small drawing of a seahorse on the face of a new Seiko watch, and then soon after got me to buy the watch. One reason for my saying that he used a watchmaker to create his sign is that around this time he got an engraver to do a small job on a compact I bought for my mother. The compact that 'said' he had put my brother in a grave (shipped him out, permanently).

The Gx1 False Fracture Diagnosis

At the start of the 1967/68 rugby season, aged nineteen, I had started to play rugby again (I hadn't played the game since I left school). I played for the college I was studying part time at, Llandaff Tech. The college just had the one team, playing adult (over 19) fixtures in the Cardiff area. Gx1 did not hit me in this season. He didn't mind my playing the game as long as it was low level rugby. However at the end of the season it was once again obvious to him that my rugby was about to cause problems for the plans he had. I was elected captain of the team for the next season.

I didn't know it at the time but the fixture lecturer at the college had plans for me to play for Cardiff rugby club.

In May 1968 Gx1 already had his Jersey murder plan in place (which he had formed four or five months earlier) to stop me going to university in September 1968, now, it was apparent to him, that his plan would serve a second purpose, it would also stop my progress in rugby.

But, disaster for Gx1, his attempt to kill me in Jersey in August 1968 failed. He stopped me going to university by other means but he was still stuck with the rugby problem.

What he did here was one of his most vile hits. It is difficult to rate them, say which is the worst, they are all in the despicable category. His mind was warped to the extreme.

In the second game of the 1968/69 season, about 10th September, he arranged to have a false 'hairline fracture of an ankle' hospital diagnosis attached to me. This, for Gx1, would do the job of stopping my rugby for a while (plaster on the lower half of my left leg) but it would not mean a permanent stop on my rugby.

He didn't want a permanent stop on my rugby (a fracture of a leg/ankle bone that goes right across the bone, means a permanent stop) because when he shipped me to Australia he had decided that I could play rugby there (with my brother being a keen rugby man).

After two months the plaster was taken off my ankle, and in theory I could return to playing rugby straightaway. But I didn't because I thought I should make sure my ankle would be okay when I started playing again by giving it more time to strengthen, and I did not play for the rest of the 1968/69 season.

The sign that Gx1 attached to this false fractured ankle hit, a 'sign' that 'advertised' what was about to happen, is the greyhound sign. It's detailed in TCF25, in the section that starts on page 63. I was the potential Arms Park greyhound (Arms Park is Cardiff's ground), the winger in the Cardiff side. There was a greyhound track around the perimeter of the ground, it was in use every week. The sign said it was going to be a bullet, lead, in my head to weigh me down on one side. And the lead, the weight on one side, appeared soon after the sign (which was in the form of a joke), the plaster on my left leg, a result of the false diagnosis, which stopped my rugby.

The McCarthy 'Sign'

With his two attempts to kill me having failed Gx1 stopped me going to university in September 1968 using his covert influence. And he inserted one of his signs here. It 'said' that he had stopped me going to university because I was a commie.

Instead of enrolling on a full time university course in 1968 I found myself starting a new job. An electronics technician at a hospital in Cardiff. And Gx1 created the sign by finding a Mr McCarthy, who was about my age, to start at the same time as me.

The word McCarthy was/is linked to the early 1950s when the people that ran the USA used Senator McCarthy to make big anti-commie noises, speeches. Gx1 was aware of this of course because, as a covert policeman in this country, his work, his way of thinking, was anti-commie. Hence his use of the word McCarthy.

The pages 73 to 82 in TCF25 talk about this area.

A Lad Murdered by Gx1

It was 1969/70. My father was working for a small building company. They had a carpenter who had a son and daughter, both in the thirteen/fourteen area. I had met them when me and my father did a small roof job on their parents house in Penarth. One day, not long after we met, my father told me that the carpenter's son had died of a brain haemorrhage when walking near his home.

I have no doubt in saying that this was arranged by Gx1. Why did he do it? In the mind of Gx1 the lad was a worker/commie, perhaps he was doing very well at school, that would have given him a reason to hit him, keep him down, kill him. Or did he do it as a 'sign', to 'say' that he had put the poison in to me at Penarth rugby club?

I will add something here that I have not mentioned before now. In 1958 my father got a self employed plumber he knew, who was about the same age as himself, to install a new hot water tank and back boiler in our house.

One day when talking to me about the plumber my father said he was "cheap". His work was first class so he didn't mean cheap that way, what he meant was that when the plumber knew he was working for people who didn't have much money he did the work for as small a fee as possible.

My father also told me that the plumber had a son about the same age as my brother who had gone away, to live in another country. He didn't say where.

Was the plumber's son shipped out, like my brother was, by warped group x type people? Their

32

thinking being that he was a very bright son of a worker, hence a commie, and so he was to be kept down or shipped out.

The Clubhouse Meeting and the Accident

Our Llandaff Tech fixture lecturer got a female he knew who was interested in rugby, Miss W, to watch one or two of our training sessions. The idea he had was that we could start a relationship that would continue through to when I played for Cardiff. But the Gx1 'hair line fracture' hit in the second game of the 1968/69 season stopped me playing the game, and I was out for the rest of the season, which means the relationship never had a chance to start.

In about April 1969 me and DC (my rugby mate) went to a Cardiff rugby club home game. We hadn't been to a Cardiff game for ages (we stopped going regularly to Cardiff games in September 1967 when we started to play for Llandaff Tech). In the clubhouse bar after the game I saw Miss W. She was with someone (a male) so I didn't go over to her to say hello.

Also in the bar was one of the lads who played for the Llandaff Tech team, Mr V. DC and I of course talked with him and a couple of his friends. Me and DC left at about 5pm. He stayed there with his friends.

It was two or three months on when I next met Mr V. He told me that later on that night, after we met in the Cardiff clubhouse bar, he had an accident in his car and a woman in another car was killed. The accident took place near the Plaza cinema.

In the 1980s, when I was aware of Gx1 and his covert dirt activities, I looked closer at this clubhouse meeting and the accident. One of the first things that made me look closer was the fact that Australia Road was about three hundred yards from the Plaza (the Plaza is not there now). The accident occurred, it seems, on the stretch of road, a main road, running between the Australia Road junction and the Plaza.

Australia Road was, of course, for Gx1, what it was all about. He had 'ship out' plans for me, one way.

It appears that Gx1 was into this clubhouse bar meeting and the meeting I had later with Mr V. 'A woman was killed near Australia Road'. A fatal car accident is rare enough but here it was near Australia Road? It had to be Gx1 'saying' something. And there is only one thing he could have been 'saying', Miss W was 'dead'. Meaning that I would not be going to her and Cardiff rugby club.

Was there a car accident? In the 1980s I thought there was, and that Gx1 had arranged it, with the 'woman was killed bit' fed into Mr V, i.e. it was a lie that he believed. Could be, but these days my thoughts on this are a bit different. I think it is more likely that Gx1 somehow got Mr V to tell me he'd had an accident and a woman was killed when he never did. Lie to me in other words.

The last time I saw Mr V was when he told me about the accident. So I have never asked him about what he said.

Details of this clubhouse bar meeting and the accident meeting are in TCF25, in the section that starts on page 147.

Poisoned By Gx1 Before the Cardiff Rugby Club Trial

So the 1969/70 season was approaching. And at the start of August '69 I joined Cardiff rugby club for training twice a week in the evenings. This would lead to a trial with the club just before the season started.

Gx1 was watching me closely. The situation meant that I could become a player with Cardiff, something that was entirely against what he wanted. As from years earlier he knew that if influential rugby people got hold of me they could form rugby plans for me in this country and that would ruin his 'ship out' plan.

What I said in the last chapter tells you that Gx1 had already, before I started training with Cardiff, formed plans to stop me playing for them, i.e. Miss W and the club were 'dead' as far as I was concerned.

In the end of August trial game Gx1 arranged to have me poisoned/doped in the hours before it took place. The result was that when I got onto the field I found that I was semi-useless. I couldn't run.

The trial was in ten minute sessions and after one session I was taken off the field and not selected to stay on at the club. There is no doubt that the Cardiff selectors did not suspect that I had been poisoned/doped, they presumably thought that things looked odd but the idea of doping players to fix them, stop them, was not present in these years.

About two weeks before this trial poisoning Gx1 gave out another 'dead' rugby 'sign'. My car's number plate (which he had recently arranged for me to purchase) had the name of a funeral home on it (in

Gx1 language, pgn). He called at our house one day and he wanted to look at the new car. I went with him to the car which was outside the house. He specifically referred to the number plate on the boot. This was to 'tell me' that my boot(s) were in a funeral home, i.e. top level rugby, Cardiff rugby club, was, for me, 'dead'. Details on this 'sign' are in TCF25, in the section that starts on page 64.

I will add something here that I didn't include in TCF25. It is in earlier editions of TCF. On this number plate visit Gx1, before we looked at the car, told me that he had a number of old Autocar magazines that I could have. I never got them.

This was another Gx1 'sign'. My brother's initials are CRT. There is a crt in Autocar. There is also an obvious u to in the word. He was 'telling me' 'u to CRT'. He had plans to ship me out, one way, to live with my brother and his family in Australia. And that, in his warped mind, meant top level rugby for me in this country was 'dead'.

I will tell you about something here that I was aware of in the 1980s and I have become more sure that I am right in recent years. At Cardiff rugby club in 1967/68 Gerald Davies was playing as a centre. And he also played for the welsh team. Well our fixture lecturer at the college I was playing rugby for in 1967/68 (Llandaff Tech), had formed the idea that my going to Cardiff rugby club was the thing for me to do. I could play alongside Gerald and perhaps this would get me into the welsh team.

In 1968 Gx1 knew about our fixture lecturer's plans, he knew, with the false fracture diagnosis and then this trial poisoning, that he was destroying what was expected to be a top level rugby career for me.

The Gx1 Car Theft and On Call Job

In March 1971 it was time for Gx1 to start the 'ship out' process. He used his position to arrange for me to start a job at St Bartholomew's hospital in London. The next step, after a year or so at the hospital, would be a plane from London to Australia (one way).

Well, quite naturally in my mind, when I moved to London I carried on playing rugby. First at Central London Polytechnic (where I was studying part-time) and then at Sudbury Court rugby club in north west London where, in August, I took part in their pre 1971/72 season training. Gx1 didn't mind this because it was low level rugby, and he had no objection to my playing at that level.

I had moved to a flat in north west London that a friend of mine had bought. He had played for the Llandaff Tech rugby team. It was his idea that we went to the nearby Sudbury Court rugby club.

It soon became apparent to Gx1 that my rugby was again big trouble for him. Sudbury Court, a week or so before the season started, had pushed me to the nearby Wasps rugby club. And in the Wasps first game of the season I played for their second team, had a faultless game, and scored. In the next game I again played in the second team and had another faultless game. They wanted me to play in the first team.

I have previously said (in TCF25) that Gx1, as soon as he knew the club wanted me to play in the first team, covertly arranged with someone at the club to get me moved down to the third team and then the fourth team. Yes that could well be the case (he was certainly in contact with someone at the club), but there is something that took place at this time that, it now seems, was the initial cause of my not moving into the first team. My car was stolen.

I was training with the Wasps in the evening twice a week. Every work day, Mon-Fri, I drove at 8am from where I was living in Sudbury to Wembley where I parked the car and got the train to my job at Bart's.

One day I returned to the car at 6-15pm to find that it had been stolen. I am not sure what day this was but if it was a training day my rugby kit would have been in the boot (I drove straight from here to the Wasps ground). Without the car I couldn't get to the Wasps so I didn't train that evening.

Gx1 had presumably been told that if a player didn't attend the mid-week evening training sessions he would not be selected for the first or second teams. So he arranged the theft to stop my evening training at the Wasps. No car meant no training sessions and no first or second team for me, it was as simple as that.

This car theft could have taken place in the week following the second game I played for the Wasps second team, i.e. the club wanted me in the first team for the next game and so he immediately arranged the theft to stop me attending the training.

Without the car I didn't go to evening training for two weeks or so. But then it was found by the police and returned to me (no damage to it). So, I don't recall exactly, my evening training must have resumed, but only for perhaps one week because Gx1 quickly thought up a new way to stop my training.

This was more Gx1 dirt. In October he arranged for the head of my department at Bart's to put me into an on call job at the hospital, and to do the job I had to move to a flat that was near the hospital. So I moved out of my friends flat near the Wasps ground in Sudbury to a flat in east central London. This made me stop going to the Wasps for the twice a week evening training. Well I thought that driving at rush hour time from east central London to Sudbury in north west London was not on. And there was no tube station close to the Wasps ground.

The so called 'on call' job at Bart's was rubbish (totally unnecessary). And the head of my department must have known it when he told me to take the job. He was simply doing what Gx1 (or his contact man) had told him to do.

For the first week or so in the on call job the hospital switchboard called me two or three times to attend an emergency admission (car accidents etc). But then they stopped calling me, they knew my presence, an electronics technician, wasn't necessary. Their initial calls were a result of their being told to give me the impression that I was required.

Within two weeks of starting the on call job I had realised it was pointless. Why had the head of my department put me into such a job? I could not understand it.

I was doing a normal electronics job in the day in the electronics department, which was okay, and this is presumably why I never went to the head of the department to ask him why he had put me into the on call job. I just got on with the normal job and ignored the fact that I was supposedly also on call.

The thought never entered my head that the head of my department had put me into the on call job to make me move from Sudbury so as to stop my evening training at the Wasps, i.e. to stop me playing for their first team.

By the spring of 1972 I was looking for a new job. Then in June 1972 I left Bart's to go to Australia.

The Diamond Appears Again

It is September 1971. I was at the Wasps rugby club in north west London. I was playing in their second team and they wanted me to play in their first team.

Gx1 did not want me to play for the first team and he, as detailed in the last chapter, arranged some hits that would stop me playing for the first team.

Arranging these hits was a busy time for him. And, as he often did, he thought up a sign to go with them. The sign was the title of a song and a film, "Diamonds are Forever". The film first appeared in cinemas in December 1971. His high level government position (in MI5) meant that he was able to influence people in many areas.

A diamond, in his mind, referred to the May 1960 baseball game in which he hit me, with the intention of stopping me proceeding, in the following years, to the Cardiff Boys and Wales Boys rugby teams. Hence, in saying diamonds are forever, he was saying that when he had killed my top level rugby in 1960, it meant that it was 'dead' forever. His recent September 1971 hit arrangements had ensured that I did not play for the Wasps first team.

I talk about the 1960 baseball game in "The Diamond Hit" chapter, earlier in this book.

Gx1 Stops My Relationship
with Miss L

In this chapter and the next three chapters I talk about four very good females I was in contact with when I was working in London (March 1971 to June 1972). I had a short romantic relationship with three of them.

Miss L was the best friend of my rugby mate's girlfriend. His girlfriend had introduced me to her in 1970 in Cardiff when she got her to join the three of us at a pub. I was going with Miss N at the time so we just said hello, became friends.

In March 1971 I started the job in London and about three weeks later it was made known to me that Miss L had started work at a London hospital. Did she move to London because I was there? The answer seems to be yes. Because after I contacted her she invited me out on a number of occasions (sometimes she had a girlfriend with her). However I was still 'going with' Miss N and so our meetings were on a 'friends only' basis.

In September 1971 Miss N and I stopped seeing each other (she was in Cardiff). This meant that I wasn't going with anyone. So of course it looked like Miss L would be my new girlfriend. She liked the fact that I was a rugby player, it had helped to encourage her to move to London in the first place. And now, September 1971, I was playing rugby at the Wasps, which of course increased her interest in me. And Miss N was not now 'in the way'. This meant that our 'just friends' relationship was about to change to an involved/romantic relationship. Exactly what she wanted. And what happened next? She left her steady hospital job and started work as an air hostess! A job that would make it more difficult for us to meet. It doesn't make sense.

I'd say, knowing that Gx1 was around and fixing things, that he used his covert influence to make her change jobs as a first step in stopping the relationship (he did the same three months later with Miss P).

In January 1972 Gx1, using his usual dirt methods, stopped my relationship with Miss L. But I didn't know this at the time. On what was in fact our the last night out we parted on very good terms. The Gx1 finish was done by using smears he got applied to me after this night out. The fact that I did not see her again was, I thought, because she was out of the country.

The Gx1 Stop Sex Poison

It was November 1971 and I was playing rugby at the Wasps (Gx1 had ensured that I did not play for the first team and got me pushed down to the fourth team). The fact that I was at the Wasps had it seems caused Miss H to move from Cardiff to a job at a London hospital.

We had first met in Cardiff in 1969, and I went out with her for one night. This was the night Gx1 leaked the engine oil in the car I was driving, hence the car was put out of action and our first night out ruined. In other words Gx1 was successful in stopping the relationship. But she nevertheless still appreciated me because, as I say, she somehow made it known to me in November 1971 that she had moved to London.

I actually thought that she was a very good female. I couldn't really understand why I hadn't asked her out again after the ruined night out in Cardiff. But I supposed it was because my car was laid up, off the road, for three or more weeks after the leaked oil night.

Anyway as soon as I knew she was working in a London hospital I phoned the place, spoke to her and we arranged a night out.

Gx1 was of course all along closely monitoring my life, he didn't want anything to get in the way of his ship out plan. Miss H was a 'non ship out' female. In other words Gx1 was out to ensure my second night out with her was also ruined.

He apparently expected us to proceed toward sex when we got back to her place. He arranged for a drink I had at the pub we went to, which was not far from the house she was staying at, to be poisoned/doped. Well either that or he got the poison given to me in the hours before I met her, when I was still at Bart's (the hospital I worked at). The poison made it impossible for me to have sex with her.

I thought she was very good, and she obviously liked me, our drink at the pub had been fine, and when we got back to her place we proceeded toward sex (there was no one else in the house). But I felt odd, there was no hard on at all for me, I could not understand it, nothing like it had ever happened before. I left her at about 11pm feeling like a bit of an idiot, and feeling like that meant I did not ask her out again.

I prefer to use the word poison instead of dope because, as I have said at some other time, any substance that is given to a person to adversely effect his natural bodily system is, as far as I am concerned, a poison.

The use of poisons by government officials, perhaps via an unofficial hit man, has to be one of the vile aspects of their work. I think they try not to use the word poison preferring to use dope instead. On the basis that 'I got him doped' sounds milder than 'I got him poisoned'.

A Night South of London

Miss P was a nurse at Barts. I met her one evening a week or so before Christmas 1971. I didn't see Miss L at all in the weeks before Christmas because of her change of job, which took her out of the country.

Then on Christmas eve lunchtime Miss P and I, with a girlfriend of her's, walked around the shops in central London. I then drove her friend to Cardiff in my car. She lived in west Wales and I took her to Cardiff train station to get the train home.

On my return to Bart's after the Christmas break I found that Miss P wanted me to go with her to her parents home, which was about twenty miles south of London, on a Saturday, stay the night, and return to London on Sunday. Well I thought she was a decent female, so I of course said yes.

On the Saturday we drove there in my car. Her parents were there and we got on okay. After dinner on Sunday we returned to London.

It's of interest to note that we never had sex on the trip. Sex was not that important to me. What was important was yes the way a female looked, but also the way she thought, talked, were our minds compatible? And with Miss P, she passed the test with ease.

We appeared to be getting into a permanent relationship and for Gx1 this was no good at all. Within days of our trip he arranged for her to move out of the hospital flat (where we could easily meet with my living near the hospital) to a place in central London. And, within another week or two, he got her to leave the Bart's job and move to a hospital in Oxford. This finished our relationship. Exactly what he wanted.

We met one more time. It was April/May 1972. I had applied for a job with an electronics company based in Slough and after the interview I drove to Oxford to meet her (I had phoned her to arrange it). We met in her room at the hospital. Here Gx1 gave a covert 'sign' that said 'hop it', 'shove off', 'the relationship is going nowhere'.

We were in her room for an hour or so then we drove to a pub on the outskirts of Oxford, stayed there for perhaps an hour, then at about 9pm I dropped her off at the hospital and drove to London. Our relationship was fine when we parted. This was the last time we met.

Gx1 Stops the Wasps Female

In about February 1972, someone at the Wasps, a committee man or similar, knowing that I was playing in the fourth team when really I should be playing in the first team decided he was going to try to change things. He was going to do this by getting me to start a relationship with a female he knew, Miss R. Then, with the relationship proceeding, he would be able to say, 'with a girlfriend he is all set for playing in our first team'.

Gx1 was in on what was going on, quite obviously he was against my starting with Miss R. He used his usual covert dirt activities to ensure I did not start a relationship with her.

Gx1 Hits a Passenger Ship

In April 1972 my brother and his family moved into a newly built house. This was accommodation that was suitable for my arrival, and Gx1 knew it of course, and he got me to buy a ticket for Australia. The ticket was a one way ticket that was by air from London to Singapore and from there by ship to Perth, then air to Adelaide. The ship would take eight days to get to Perth.

I intended to be back in Britain in September 1972 for my rugby mate's wedding, so why I bought a one way ticket is odd in natural thinking terms. I had enough money to buy a return but spent some of it on a couple of expensive purchases, which left me with only enough for a one way ticket. It could be that Gx1 got the idea fed to me, by one or two people where I worked, that I could get a job in Australia and hence earn money for the return ticket.

In early June I boarded a plane at London Gatwick for a flight to Singapore. Once there it was straight from the plane to the ship.

Three or was it four days out the ship developed a list. I awoke one morning to find that it was leaning over at about twenty six degrees, perhaps it was a bit less. I went on deck and saw that the ship was proceeding in a calm sea.

Well, well. For me it was, 'weigh him down on one side using a piece of lead'. Any connection? I have no doubt that the list was a result of Gx1 activities. Well it must have been Gx1, how could I be on a 'weighed down on one side ship' when a severe list happens to perhaps one ship in 500,000?

We, the passengers, were told that a water tank in the ship had fractured and that the showers could only be used for one hour per day.

Gx1 got one of his hit men (MI5/6) to create a fracture in the boat's main water tank or in a ballast tank. This caused water to leak into the bottom of the ship and hence the list. The tank must have been placed to one side of the ship.

The ship diverted to the nearest port, Geraldton, which was about 260 miles north of Perth. When we got there water was pumped on to the ship to level it up and we continued to Perth.

Why did he do it? What was he 'saying'?

I have made some comments relating to the question I have just asked in TCF25, page 93/4. I will now look at it from a different angle.

Gx1 saw Geraldton on the map of Australia and he connected it to Gerald Davies.

In 1968 our fixture lecturer for the Llandaff Tech rugby team had me on course for playing alongside Gerald in the Cardiff rugby club team (I didn't know this at the time). Gx1 put an end to this, made sure I did not play for Cardiff, by using his false hairline fracture diagnosis in September 1968, then, at the start of the next season he got me poisoned.

For Gx1 it was, "your rugby at the top level in this country is dead". But it seems (from other signs), that he had the intention of letting me play rugby in Australia, perhaps without being kept down, hit. So, in connecting me to Gerald in Australia he was saying that I could take up my rugby from where I left off in 1968.

The Gx1 Ship Out Date

So in June 1972, two months after the end of my season with the Wasps, I arrived in Australia. I moved in to my brother's place.

This, as I have said, was three months before DC, who was my rugby mate until 1969, was due to get married in Gloucestershire. I was to be the best man at his wedding.

It would seem that Gx1 made a big mistake here. How was I going to stay in Australia, permanently, when, in September 1972, I wanted to be at my rugby mate's wedding?

If he had shipped me out after the wedding he presumably would have had no, or at least much less, difficulty in keeping me in Australia.

His thinking could have gone like this. He knew that there was pressure in the Wasps for me to play in the first team. If I was still in London in September 1972, the start of the new rugby season, he could find that the pressure could be increased. This is assuming that I had managed to return to my two evenings a week training at the club (which Gx1 had stopped in September 1971).

So by shipping me out months before the 1972/73 season began he avoided being stuck with new rugby problems.

He probably also thought that I lacked interest in being at DC's wedding. This was because in January 1969, when DC started to go out with the female who was to be his wife, we had stopped going out with each other (we stopped playing rugby together when Gx1 hit me in September 1968), meaning that from that time on we had seen very little of each other. But he was wrong here, rugby had made me and DC very good mates and even though I hadn't seen him for quite a while it was important for me to be at his wedding.

The Gx1 'Stop the Return Flight' Poison

It was the end of August 1972 when I left my brother's place and went to Sydney for a plane to London. At about 6pm I booked into a hotel in Sydney ready for my flight out the following morning.

Gx1 knew that I intended to be at DC's wedding and he was going to use his connections, which he presumably had with the Australian security services, to make me stay where I was, in Australia.

As I booked in to the hotel the manager (I assumed he was) appeared from the reception desk office as soon as I gave the receptionist my details. He took some interest in me, he said he was from Cardiff, and we sat down for a few words in the reception area and I had a cup of tea that he offered me.

Three or four hours later I was ill. Too ill to travel. And in the morning instead of going to the airport I went to a cheaper hotel to lay up in bed, ill.

Gx1 had got me poisoned (in the tea) to keep me off the return flight.

After three days or so, feeling a bit better, I went to the airport to get on a plane. There were problems. But a day later I got on a plane for London.

I should add that I had no spare money to buy another ticket. Credit/debit cards were just starting up and I didn't have one.

Gx1 Breaks Mr HC's Leg

Well here I was, early September 1972, back in Cardiff at the start of a new rugby season, what was going to happen now? Within a couple of days of my return and re-commencing the job at the University Hospital of Wales that I'd been in before I moved to London, I was told by someone who worked in the hospital that a Cardiff Hospitals rugby team was being started up, getting fixtures in and around Cardiff. I said yes okay I'd play for it.

The team was started up because I had arrived back in Cardiff. It appears that Mr Q arranged the start up.

Mr Q had become a member of Group X in 1969 when I started to go out with his daughter, Miss N. I was still going with her at the start of my Wasps season but then we drifted apart. We didn't see each other for some months but toward the end of the season she came to London for a weekend. We did not however continue our relationship after that (we stayed on good terms).

Mr Q was a rugby man and he was very interested when he heard I was at the Wasps. He knew that they wanted me to play in their first team but that it had been blocked by Gx1. Mr Q was very unhappy about this but he couldn't do anything about it because Gx1 was senior to him (Mr Q was a policeman).

When I returned from Australia he saw his chance to put things right for me on the rugby front. He arranged for the Cardiff Hospitals rugby team to be started up as a way of getting me to Cardiff rugby club. It could be that his son, who was studying at the hospital, actually made the start up arrangements.

Gx1 was again in big trouble, for years he had my rugby in this country on stop and here was I being pushed once again toward Cardiff rugby club. Well obviously he was going to think up ways of destroying this new push. He proceeded on two lines.

I had a friend, Mr HC, who worked in the department I was in at the hospital and he was going to join me playing for the new rugby team. He was going to be my new rugby mate. Gx 1 put him in a hospital bed within hours of the start of the first game played by the team

Not long after the rugby game started Mr HC was laying on the ground with the lower part of one of his legs broken (the shin was distorted with the skin being pushed out by the broken bone). There is no doubt at all that Gx1 arranged for it to happen. Details on how this was done are in TCF25, on page 189. The first question for me to answer is 'why did he do it?'

He did it to take my rugby mate out of the game, permanently. My having a rugby mate was very helpful for me as a player, before and after games. Taking him out would remove a useful addition to my rugby, make things not so good for me. And that was the basis of all the hits he had carried out on my rugby, i.e. keep my rugby down, stop me moving on to top level rugby.

The second line Gx1 proceeded on was as follows. Here he went for the smear/dirty routine. He worked in the local council offices as you know, well it was therefore easy for him to stop the team playing on a council's parks pitch a week or so after our first game, and tell the team to use a field in a mental hospital in Cardiff where a pitch would soon be marked out.

This was a smear job on a big scale. A rugby team with it's home ground in a mental hospital! The team's integrity was destroyed, how he got the person who ran the team to agree to it I just don't know. Anyway the result was that for the rest of the 1972/73 season I was playing for a 'bit of a joke' team (when playing at home).

Someone says, 'why didn't Gx1 have your leg broken?' Well he didn't do this, in this game, or in earlier years, because he envisaged my playing rugby in Australia. So whilst I was in this country he only restricted my rugby. Yes I had returned from Australia at the start of this rugby season but he still had ideas on pushing me back there.

Now let me look at what happened to Mr HC from a different angle. If a person, in a genuine accident, is hit by a car and comes away with a broken leg he will get financially compensated for what happened. The company that insured the car would pay him a large amount in damages. I say this just to give you an idea of the area I am in. What happened to Mr HC was not a "genuine accident". A Gx1 hit man got at his shin the night before the game when he was asleep and doped. He ensured that the bone was substantially weakened so that hours later it broke when subjected to the actions of a rugby game.

This was a criminal act, damaging an important bone in a person to ensure that it soon broke. Well even if this was reported to the police soon after it happened how could they, even if they identified the hit man, have prosecuted him when he was a government hit man? Paid by the government and told what to do by Gx1, a high level government official. No, they would not have prosecuted the hit man, but would they have prosecuted Gx1? Perhaps their enquiries would have found out about a number of his vile activities. Realised he was a bent official in other words. They presumably would have stopped his vile activities. But would the prosecution service have prosecuted, in public, an MI5 employee? Doubtful. So if there was no prosecution for the criminal element in this broken shin occurrence could Mr HC get financially compensated for what was done to him? Could he get damages in a civil court in other words.

Any criminal act can be followed by a claim for damages when the criminal prosecution is successful. The reason it's not usually done is because the convicted criminal has very little money, hence a claim for money from him is pointless. In this case though, the hit man and Gx1 (his boss) were government employees, and that means the government would be liable for paying the damages, and obviously the government has money. But if the prosecution service would not prosecute a government hit man or Gx1 there would be no convicted criminal to automatically follow up with a claim for damages. Hence the only way for Mr HC to obtain damages from the government would be for him to cite an unknown government hit man as the person who did it, and then claim damages, knowing that the government knew that all of what he said was true. Would the government have come up with the damages?

There was another odd occurrence in this season with the Cardiff Hospitals team. I tell you about it in the next chapter.

Diamond Number Three

In an away game near the end of my season with the Cardiff Hospitals Gx1 got a hit man, using an electron/laser gun, to fire a beam into me. This made me fall (it felt like a 240 volt shock) when I was supposed to be making a try saving tackle on my opposing winger, and the winger ran in to score.

Gx1 knew that a Cardiff selector, or an influential person, had ideas on getting me to move to Cardiff rugby club. He got him invited to this game knowing that he was going to dirty me, make me look hopeless, to ensure I did not go to Cardiff.

Hence Cardiff rugby club was not pushed in front of me as a next step in my rugby career.

Gx1 chose this particular game for the invite and the hit because it gave him one of his signs (which he often attached to his covert dirt activities). The game was played on a field known as the Diamond ground. In other words his 1960 'diamond hit', which was intended to 'kill' any significant success for me with my rugby, was going to be repeated.

The MGB

In May 1973 I bought a second hand MGB from a car repair garage in Cardiff (near the Three Horse Shoes etc). It was about four years old and in good condition. I sold it in 1974.

It was 1979 when I started to realise that it was Gx1 who had been creating problems for me in earlier years, and sometime later I realised that he often placed covert signs into his arrangements. Were there Gx1 covert signs in the MGB? Probably. And I tried to figure them out.

Morris I got early on, the name connected to the Morris in the Penarth rugby game when Gx1 had me hit, kept down, to stop me playing for the first team (MGB is Morris Garages model B). This hit took place a couple of weeks after he'd got me poisoned in the hours before the Cardiff rugby club trial game, to ensure I did not play for them. But the number plate on the car I could not connect to anything. And today I don't think he used the number plate as a sign.

In about 2000 I picked up on the car's colour. It was again a 'you to Australia' sign. I will explain.

In the 1980s, I was casually calling the car orange, which didn't mean much to me. But to be more exact the bodywork of the car, the paint, was actually called bronze, or bronze yellow (I bought small spray paint tins for the car). Well the word bronze had an obvious connection. In 1963 I got a bronze medal award. Gx1 had arranged the award to pin a label on me that said, 'you are on a long walk to Australia'. In this car purchase he was no doubt saying that I could play rugby in Australia (but I could not play top level rugby in Britain).

Yes the electron/laser beam fired into me when I was playing for the Cardiff Hospitals team (as in the last chapter) was, once again, to stop me going to Cardiff rugby club. If I had proceeded on that route a decent female would have to be placed in front of me, to start a relationship with her (I didn't have a girlfriend at the time). But with that route having been blocked by Gx1 the decent female placement didn't happen.

And what did happen? Within weeks of being hit by the electron/laser beam Gx1 got me put on to the MGB, with it's 'you can play rugby in Australia' sign. And at the same time he got Mr E to place Miss D in front of me (the meal at his place). Gx1 knew she was trouble, and that he could ship her out, with me, on a one way ticket to Australia that he again had me lined up for.

But in my natural thinking terms I wasn't in the least bit interested in starting a relationship with her. She was not at all my type.

Gx1 didn't like my turning down his choice of a female and a few months later, when I was about to leave the hospital job, he again got Miss D pushed in front of me. This time he arranged for the woman she worked with to give me a big, 'she likes you', talk, coupled to the, 'innocent church going girl', stuff. Somehow, against my natural thoughts, I decided to give it a try, have a closer look at her. I asked her out and she said yes.

Back to the MGB. Gx1 did not just happen to see a bronze MGB that would fit his sign activities, and get me directed to it. He got the car sprayed bronze in the week or two before I bought it. I can say this, without any doubt at all, because about three weeks before I bought the car I had seen it at a car sales place just outside Cardiff. It was white.

I was looking for a second hand MGB in my price range and there was only a few around. When I went to look at the MGB on sale at the car repair garage I saw that it was the same car I had looked at three weeks earlier, but now it wasn't white, it was bronze. It was presumably priced lower than when I'd seen it before and because of this I bought it.

This car spray job is just one of the things Gx1 could arrange from his high level government position. Some of his arrangements are surprising, others, many others, were criminal offences and vile.

The Gx1 Plan to Murder My Father

In August 1973 the Gx1 plan to murder my father went into effect. He got a hit man to knife my father when he was asleep and doped. The knifing, the bleeding, was made out as a 'natural occurrence', i.e. apart from the bleeding my father was unharmed, and no foul act was suspected. He went into hospital in Cardiff (the UHW) where Gx1 had a false diagnosis of cancer ready for him.

The plan was to kill him using poison some time later, with 'natural occurrence' again being applied (cancer), hence there would be no questions asked. A quiet, covert, murder.

Details on the Gx1 murder plan are in TCF25, pages 98/100. What I will do in this chapter is go over parts of it paying particular attention to some of the 'signs' that Gx1 attached to his plan.

In 1956 Gx1 had told my father that he could arrange for him to get a fifteen year mortgage from the council (they did mortgages on a small scale). My father said yes he would take it on. Gx1, in arranging the mortgage, had the intention to murder my father when it was finished (fully paid).

It was about 1960 when the idea of a new hospital in Cardiff was formed. It was going to be called the University Hospital of Wales (UHW). It was to be built on part of Heath park, hence it would also be known as the Heath hospital.

In 1960 Gx1 carried out a hit on me at Heath park ('the diamond hit' chapter earlier in this book). This hit served two 'sign' purposes for him. It would help to kill off my physical education teacher's, 'he is outstanding at rugby', and it would indicate that my father was going to be knifed at that place (the Heath hospital was built on the baseball field). Bowler and backstop were the relevant words for the knifing (see TCF25, section that starts on page 182).

In 1960/61 the Gx1 sheath knife sign appeared (Heath knife). I talk about it in the chapter of that name earlier in this book.

The final payment of the mortgage was due to take place in 1971. However in 1967 my father bought the freehold (the land) by increasing the remaining amount on the mortgage. The mortgage was extended by two years, this meant the final payment would be in 1973, when my father would be sixty four.

In 1967 the Beatles (a british pop music group) produced a song called "When I'm 64". This was Gx1 with one of his 'signs'. He had arranged with someone who was close to the Beatles for them to produce a song with that title. My father would be hit/murdered when he was sixty four (in 1973). My father's initials are WT, there is a T in "I'm" if you use a roman I. The song 'said' W T 64.

This was not the only time he used the Beatles for a 'sign'. In 1968 they produced a song called "The Long and Winding Road". The first line is "The long and winding road that leads to your door". My mother's first name is Dor (Doreen). The "Winding" was inserted to get my father's name into the song. "Long and Winding" is LaW, which is by father's first name in reverse (his name is Wal, short for Walby). Gx1 was 'saying', in this Beatles song, that there was a long road that led to my father's wife, i.e. it would take a few years for him to get to her (by which time, with my father dead, she would have a fully paid for house in her name).

To get, obtain, my mother, and the fully paid for house, Gx1 would have to marry her. And to do that he would first have to murder his wife, by 'accident'/ 'natural causes', of course.

In June 1973 Gx1 connected a car I bought to 'signs' that said 'the knife is going into WAT's back in 1973 and he will end up dead as a result of it'. Bier/coffin. See TCF25, page 124/5. Two months later a Gx1 hit man covertly knifed my father (when he was asleep and chloroformed).

I have more Gx1 'signs' that indicate what he was going to have done to my father at the Heath hospital to tell you about. These are the Heathway, St Malo, and Tresaith signs. Details as follows.

Earlier in this book and in TCF25 pages 198/9 I explained how the origins of this affair date back to the 1940s, the knife in the trunk. And this was the basis for Gx1 getting my father to take a mortgage on the Malefant Street house in 1956. For Gx1 Malefant meant elephant which in turn meant trunk, i.e. the knife would be going in to my father when he was living at the house.

Gx1 emphasized the knife in the Malefant Street house by getting a policeman with a surname of Dart to move into a house that was a hundred yards up the street from our house. Dart, in british surnames, is probably as close as you can get to 'knife'. The policeman had a son about my age and we got to know each other. Hence Mr Dart, the knife, was connected to me and hence connected to my father, the knife was going in to my father.

In 1963 Gx1 'improved' on this dart sign. This was when he moved the policeman to a house two and a half miles away, in Heathway.

The policeman's son, a week or so before he moved from Malefant Street, invited me and two friends that lived near me, to his house in Heathway once a week to play board games. This went on for three or four winter months.

This new sign 'advertised' where my father was going to be knifed. The "way" in Heathway gives WAT, my father, (the T is in the Y). Heath gives the Heath hospital, which was starting to be built at this time. In other words the knifing, the surgical knifing, was going to take place at the Heath hospital (a week or two after the covert knifing).

Gx1 saw that he could give even more information in this dart sign. Heathway is a long road and toward one end of it St Malo Road joins it. He got the policeman to buy a house near this junction. St Malo 'said' that the knife in the trunk was going to take the form of a knife into my father's rectum.

St Malo (in France) 'said' this because it is on an estuary and in 1961 a decision was made to construct a dam across it to generate electricity, i.e. for Gx1 St Malo, with it's dam on an estuary, was equivalent to a sewn up, blocked, rectum. Hence his selection of a house near St Malo Road. His taking a holiday every summer in Jersey meant that he knew, had been to, St Malo.

In August 1969 I started to go out with Mr Q's daughter, Miss N. In the summer of 1970 I stayed for a few days with her at a caravan her parents had in Tresaith, west Wales.

This was a Gx1 'sign'. It was to emphasize that 37 was very relevant to his activities. Tresaith is welsh for 37. He planned to knife my father in 1973 in the back. 37 backwards.

In other words Gx1 got Mr Q, in the months after I started going out with his daughter, to buy a caravan in Tresaith.

Gx1 used 37 a few times to indicate the importance of 1973. Tresaith, and also the Three Horseshoes in 1973, and junction 37 of the M4 at the end of the 1960's (details of the latter two are in TCF25, pages 124 and 144/5). It was 1967 on when he gave out all these 37's because it was 1967 when he first knew that it would be 1973 when he would be getting my father hit.

The 1973/74 Season

The Cardiff Hospitals rugby team not surprisingly folded at the start of the 1973/74 season and I found myself playing no rugby at all.

I left the job at the hospital and spent a year working with International Computers Limited. In September 1974 I left the computer job and started a full time course at Swansea university. And rugby came back into my scene.

Gx1 Uses Dirt Activities to Stop My Rugby at the Start of the 1974/75 Season

How did I manage to get onto a full time university course at Swansea in September 1974 when Gx1 was obviously against it (in 1967/68 he twice tried to kill me to stop me starting at university)? It must have been a result of Mr Q using his influence to get me to apply for a place.

Mr Q's attempts to get me to Cardiff rugby club via the Cardiff Hospitals rugby team in the 1972/73 season had failed (he didn't know why of course). He was not content with the situation and in 1974 he formed new plans to get my rugby put right.

He somehow got me to start a full time course at Swansea university in September '74, where, he assumed, I would play for their rugby team and then Swansea rugby club. Gx1 was obviously against this but he found that he had to go along with it. He knew that he could covertly insert his dirt activities into what went on at the university to get what he wanted (me out of the university and back to Cardiff to marry Miss D), with the result that Mr Q's plans would again be ruined.

As soon as the university rugby players got together at the start of the season Gx1 got me dirtied/blacked with one of the lads that ran the team. SV, a member of staff at the college, was probably involved in the process. The result was that I was not selected for the first team or the second team (which only had the occasional game anyway).

By making sure I did not play for the college Gx1

was pursuing his intention to get me stopped at the end of the academic year. Not playing for the college on a Saturday afternoon would mean I would sometimes return to Cardiff on Friday evening for the weekend. And see Miss D. He was going to use my relationship with her to get me stopped at the college so of course he wanted me back in Cardiff at weekends to keep the relationship going.

And by stopping my college rugby he was also helping to ensure I didn't go to Swansea rugby club (why go there when I couldn't even get into the college side?).

The Boot Laces

This occurrence took place in January/February 1975 when I was at Swansea university. I considered what happened here to be very odd but I didn't make anything more of it than that.

I was changing in preparation for playing a game of rugby. When I went to tighten and tie the lace on the first boot I had put on it broke. I tried to re-arrange the lace to use the longest part of it that was left but it broke again and again. The lace was useless. I tried to tie the lace on my other boot but it was also in the same useless condition. Someone had dripped acid along the entire length of both laces.

I borrowed the laces from someone's shoes (short laces) and made do with those. I played the game with loose boots.

I told you in the last chapter that Gx1 had arranged, when I started at Swansea university, to keep me out of the college rugby team. But I could still play the game. This was on a Wednesday afternoon when anyone in the college who played rugby could form teams and play against each other. This acid laces occurrence took place prior to one of these games.

What happened here was a group x language 'sign'. It said, 'your rugby is going nowhere'.

SV, presumably acting on GX1's instructions, dripped the acid on the laces (I am almost certain that it was SV that done it, I talk about him in TCF25, pages 123 and 227). He was what I would call the college's covert fix it man (or one of their covert fix it people). He could easily have got the acid from the chemistry department in the college. I put my rugby kit in a college locker at the start of the Wednesday morning lectures, he would have got at the boots during the morning using a lockers master key.

And I think that SV was involved in the forgery at the end of the academic year.

The Secretary of the Welsh
Rugby Union's Daughter

Mr Q, regardless of the fact that I somehow was
not playing for the university rugby team, was
pressing on with his plans for me to play for Swansea
rugby club. Within a couple of weeks of my starting
at the university he arranged for me to meet a friend I
knew from when I was at the UHW, Mr S. He was a
friend of Mr Q's son. We started a once a week night
out.

On perhaps our second night out he introduced
me to a girl who sometimes, with a girlfriend, joined
us, I refer to her as Miss K. A week or so later he said
that she was the daughter of the secretary of the
Welsh Rugby Union. I didn't really believe him, but I
didn't say this. I was wrong, he was correct.

Gx1 Feeds in Dirt

In February 1975 Gx1 was told that it looked like me and Miss K were going to start a relationship together. If this happened it would be a disaster for him because it would mean I would finish with Miss D and that would mean he would not be able to use her to get me stopped at Swansea university.

And if I finished with Miss D it would also mean that his 'ship out' plan, for me with her when married to her, would be scrapped.

Miss K was not a ship out female. If I started with her I would be on a standard 'stay in this country' route.

This situation troubled Gx1 a lot. After years spent keeping me down, in preparation for shipping me out, destroying a top level rugby career in the process, here I was on the point of beating him and his covert dirt activities. If I started with Miss K it would also mean I would play for Swansea rugby club (her father was closely connected to the club).

Gx1 must have been fuming. He thought up new dirt activities that were aimed at stopping a me and Miss K relationship.

The Easter break was due in the coming weeks and he decided to use it to start his new round of dirt activities.

The address of the place I was living at in Swansea had been given to me by the college accommodation office in September. About two weeks before Easter Gx1 told the accommodation office to get me out of the place.

I had intended to stay in Swansea for the three

week break but because of a slight disagreement with the landlord (contrived) I had to vacate the place days before Easter. This made me decide to return to Cardiff to stay at my parents house for the break and look for new accommodation in Swansea when I returned there after the break.

Getting me back to Cardiff for the break was useful for Gx1 because he could then use, 'he's come back to Cardiff, to see Miss D, he must like her'.

Then on my return to Swansea after the break he got me into a guest house, a bed and breakfast place, that was connected to the college. He was going to use the place to push/force me into marrying Miss D. If we stated we were going to get married it would stop 'me and Miss K' in it's tracks.

I was the only person staying at the place and at breakfast every day the landlady always had a lot to say to me.

It was probably my first breakfast there when she asked me if I had a girlfriend or was married. I replied saying I had a girlfriend in Cardiff. She then asked me what she did, I told her she had a clerical job at the UHW, and that was about it (Miss D was on the way out as far as I was concerned).

Well in the following day or two she picked on the girlfriend topic and said that I should marry her! I was astonished. I didn't tell her that she had said something which was absurd/ignorant because I didn't want to offend her. I just sat there in amazement. Apart from the little I had said about Miss D, she knew nothing about her, she had never even seen her.

The landlady's husband had something to do with the university (perhaps he knew SV).

Quite obviously Gx1 had recently been talking to someone in the college, and he fed in the words that I had a church going girlfriend who lived near Cardiff that I should marry. And the 'someone in the college' had got these words passed on to the landlady. And she repeated what she had been told.

Gx1 was using, 'he should marry Miss D', as a reason for getting me stopped at the college, i.e. when stopped I would return to Cardiff and marry the church going girl.

Straight after the landlady told me I should marry Miss D, or it could have been at breakfast the next day, she said that Miss D could stay at the place free for a night. Obviously now I can say I should have refused this offer from a landlady who had some odd ideas, but I didn't. Presumably again because I didn't want to offend her. On the phone I told Miss D about it and she soon arrived on the train in Swansea for a night with me at the guest house.

The night was part of the 'force him into marrying Miss D' instructions that Gx1 had got fed into the place. But it didn't come off. I had never had any intention of marrying her. On the contrary I was trying to get rid of her (quietly, for reasons stated elsewhere).

As a result of the failed Gx1 guest house 'marriage activities', during which it was apparent that I did not want to marry Miss D, a me and Miss K relationship had become even more likely. This was no good at all for Gx1 so he thought up another way of stopping me and Miss K.

This new way was the smear routine, he was going to dirty me so that Miss K would not want to start a relationship with me.

The Poisoning at 1405

I was at the guest house for two weeks then in mid-April I left there and moved in to a cheaper place, a room in a nearby house (about a half mile from the college). Mr U had a room there. He worked for a computer company, I had met him when I spent a year working with the company in Cardiff (1973/74).

When I returned to Swansea after the Easter break I had called to see him looking for accommodation and he told me about the guest house. He was a Gx1 'yes sir, no sir' man. Gx1 had put him into the place and told him to send me to the guest house.

It was now about the end of April. I hadn't seen Miss K for a couple of months and I was to meet her, and a girlfriend of her's, on a Saturday at 2pm outside a pub that was next to Swansea rugby club's ground. I didn't know why she wanted me to meet her there, I had just got a message to be there.

I thought Miss K was a very good female and I was interested in starting a relationship with her. So of course, as requested, I quite happily met her and her girlfriend outside the pub.

It's worth stating again here that I did not consider her to be the daughter of the secretary of the Welsh Rugby Union. Yes Mr S had told me that she was in that position but I thought he was sort of joking. And we didn't say any more about it. In other words my appreciation for her was based entirely on what I thought of her as a female, i.e. her position had nothing to do with it. From our friendship, which began six months earlier, she knew I liked her.

We met outside the pub a few minutes before 2pm and went in. It was crowded. Miss K and her girlfriend didn't want a drink and they went to sit with about six girls. I stood at the bar waiting to get served. I had a long wait, it was perhaps 2.05pm when I got served.

I couldn't go and sit, as the only male, with Miss K and her girlfriends, there was no room anyway, so I found a seat that was about forty feet from them. I didn't know anyone in the pub apart from Miss K and her girl friend so I sat quietly on my own. Which was okay, I didn't mind that, when they left I would leave with them.

I slowly became very hot, which made me feel uncomfortable, I was probably also perspiring. I couldn't understand why this was happening.

At about 2-25pm Miss K and her girlfriend got up and walked toward the exit. I joined them as they left. Outside the pub we stopped to talk. Miss K said they were going to watch the rugby game and they had stand tickets. They walked toward the rugby ground, and I went wherever I was going. I had not planned to go to the game, since moving to Swansea in September '74 I hadn't been to any of the Swansea rugby club games.

I thought it was an odd meeting. Why had Miss K wanted me to meet them there?

I did not realise what the reason for the meeting was. I just turned up not knowing what to expect. The reason was, it seems, that she was prepared to, wanted to, start a relationship with me. She assumed I was going to the game and they were going to join me, watch it together. She was either going to give me a stand ticket next to their tickets, or they were going to join me in the spectator standing area. And at the end of the game I would be expected to ask to see her again, i.e. start a relationship.

So what made Miss K change her mind at the last minute? The answer is Gx1 and the poison given to me by his hit man, the barman.

The poison made me hot and flushed. When I left the pub with them I had a very red face. And, looking like that, Miss K would not go to the game with me. She quickly said they had stand tickets and left me. Her intention of starting a relationship with me had ceased. Gx1's 'dirty him' covert arrangements to stop the relationship were successful.

Let's look at the situation from Miss K's point of view. She was, it seems, available, meaning that she was not in a steady relationship with a male. So she was looking for a suitable male. And that male would, if possible, be a rugby player. She had been told that I was a good rugby player and that I had spent a season at the Wasps. So it followed that I could be a suitable male for her. She had also been told that I had a girlfriend in Cardiff, and, that I did not appear to be particularly interested in her. And that, most probably, was about all she knew.

Mr Q had got me introduced to Miss K via his son and his friend Mr S. He did this because he was a rugby man and he knew that the Wasps had wanted me to play in their first team (I had played in their second team) and that Gx1 had stopped it happening (using covert dirt activities). And getting me to play at Swansea rugby club was a way for him to put my rugby right (correct the wrongs that had been done to me at the Wasps by Gx1). And he brought Miss K into the situation because he happened to know that she was available (and connected to Swansea rugby club).

Did Mr Q know that Gx1 had stopped me going to Cardiff rugby club in 1969 by getting me poisoned prior to a trial game I had with them? Did he know that in 1968 Gx1 had got me hit to stop my rugby (for six months)?

I said this some years back. I will repeat it here. As far as I'm concerned any substance that is covertly given to a person that is meant to adversely affect his his normal bodily process is a poison.

Diamond Number Four

One day Mr U introduced me to Mr Basey who was living in a house a couple of doors away from where we were living.

Gx1 had put Mr Basey in place for his sign purposes. The sign he had decided to use again for his hit activities was the diamond sign. The song "Diamonds are Forever" was sung by Shirley Bassey, so obviously, in the mind of Gx1, Mr Basey connected to Miss Bassey, and the connection said, 'your rugby is dead forever'.

In arranging the sign Gx1 was referring to my meeting with Miss K outside the pub, which took place at this time. He was saying, 'your rugby, via Miss K, is dead'.

The Forged Papers Examination

It was probably May when Gx1 arranged for me to be given forged/altered question papers in the end of academic year examinations for one of the subjects (two three hour examinations), to ensure I was failed in the subject. This was part of his long term thinking (formed in about 1945), which was 'keep down workers because they are commies'. He wanted me out of Swansea 'failed' and back in Cardiff where I'd get my relationship with Miss D (who lived near Cardiff) going properly (I had in fact been quietly trying to get rid of her since I'd been in Swansea). He wanted me married to her because she was a 'ship out' female and could be shipped with me to Australia.

The fixed/forged examination papers arrangement was, as usual, accompanied by a Gx1 'sign'. In this case it's two signs, both based on 66. I will tell you about them.

The two invigilators, one in each examination, committed criminal offences. Section 6 of the 1913 Forgery Act said it was an offence to use, give out, documents that the person so doing knew to be forged/false documents. So section 6 was violated twice. This gave 66, Miss D (her parents flat, where she lived, was number 66). So the 'sign' said it was Miss D for me, i.e. out of Swansea 'failed' and back to Cardiff.

In 2020 I first gave you details of the 1945 knife in the trunk (TCF25, 6th edition page 197). Well the second sign, the second connection to this 66 forgery, is the knife in the trunk. This is where Gx1 first obtained the 66, because the knife is more accurately called an indian dagger (the gg giving the 66).

So Gx1, in getting the two university lecturers to give me the forged documents, was 'saying' that he was knifing me. It was one of his arrangements that were intended to ensure I did not go on to a second year at the university.

There is no doubt at all that Gx1 arranged the forgery. Because only he knew that Miss D lived at a 66, and, that the 66 was the knife in the trunk. And, being an ex-policeman and in MI5, he had some knowledge of the 1913 Forgery Act with it's section 6.

He got at least two people in the university to carry out the forged document activities (the two invigilators who gave me the forged documents, one of them could also have made the forged documents). Three people if it was another person that made the forged documents. Four if he got someone in the administration offices to arrange all of it. In other words Gx1 was the director in a criminal conspiracy that possibly involved five people (including himself).

The police know who used, gave, the forged documents to me. They presumably also know, having confirmed they have the forged documents (but said no more), who made them.

When I had done both the examinations the belief I had was that in the first examination a question paper headed correctly but with the wrong questions on it had been given to all the students. And the invigilator either:

(i) saw the error but ignored it (expected us to get on with the examination regardless), or

(ii) did not notice the error till perhaps the end of the examination or later.

And then in the second examination (some days later), the students, all the students, were given a question paper that had been put together to take into account the mistake that had been made in the preparation of the first examination question paper.

When I went to see one of the lecturers straight after the examination results were published in the college (he had invigilated the first examination), he told me what I expected him to say, that a mistake had been made in the preparation of the question papers. He then went on to say that ten percent had been added on to all the answer papers to make up for it, and that my fail result stood. I was not happy with this but didn't do any more about it.

In September it was apparent that I could not continue at the university. My 'failure' in the forged documents subject was the reason given to me.

Now, for the first time, I had become aware of Group X activities. I felt sure that the examination irregularities that had taken place months earlier and the fact that I had been stopped at the university were a result of their influence.

Group X was three or four people outside of the university (I didn't call them "Group X" at this time, I did that years later when I started writing a book on it). As far as I was concerned it was obvious they wanted me to marry Miss D. Getting me back to Cardiff (and out of UCS) would make it happen (they were pushing/forcing me into marrying her). I also felt sure that my getting a degree was too much for them. Me, a worker, get a degree? No, that wasn't on.

When I started giving you details of this affair I used the word "hit" to label many of Gx1's vile activities, and I defined 'a hit' as being any act that someone covertly does/arranges that is intended to adversely affect another person.

In recent years, since telling you about the knife in the trunk, I have also been using the phrase, "put the knife in". It's an informal phrase that is not being used in a literal sense (it's an idiom). It is much the same as "put the poison in". When a person 'puts the knife in' (or 'puts the poison in') he is doing something covertly that is intended to adversely affect someone, and therefore it can also be called 'a hit', e.g. covertly arranging to have a false hairline fracture of an ankle diagnosis given to me was 'putting the knife in' and a 'hit'.

The Car 66 'Sign'

Here is a 'sign' given out by Gx1 in September 1975 that is in effect more confirmation that it was he that arranged the forgery four months earlier. He used Miss D and her connection to 66 again.

The car I had was causing me problems, it was off the road at times. A person in the house I was living at, Mr U (he was a Gx1 contact man), told me that there was a very good old car for sale at a car repair place in Swansea. It was for sale at a very cheap price. I went to look at it and bought it.

The car was a Sprint 2600 made by Alfa Romeo. In the name of the car you can easily see sprint and 26. Which, in the mind of Gx1, who covertly arranged for me to buy the car, meant run fast to 66, to Miss D (she lived in a 66).

I bought this car a couple of days before I was told by staff at Swansea university that I could not continue there. In other words Gx1 knew he had arranged to get me stopped and the car 'sign' was to say what I was to do next. Leave Swansea and return to Cardiff to take up my relationship with Miss D

For some time now I had known that Miss D was not for me. I had my doubts about her when I first started to go out with her. And in 1974 I became sure that I had to finish with her. But I couldn't do a quick, immediate stop, finish, without a good reason for finishing, because if I did I felt sure I'd get hit (find myself in trouble in some way). So I went for a quiet, fade out of the relationship, finish. And I thought my move to Swansea in September 1974 would do this.

On some weekends I returned to my parents house in Cardiff and when I did I went out with her in the evening. But these were infrequent meetings and we never had any sort of long term plans in place. Which meant in the weeks between our meetings I assumed she was going out with some other male, or looking for another one anyway. And I was expecting at any time for her to tell me she was going out with someone else and had finished with me. Which as I say is what I wanted.

Let me add something here. In March 1971, when I moved to London to start a job there, I was going out with Miss N. We never had any sort of long term plans in place, but anyway we kept the relationship going till September 1971, at which point I stopped going to Cardiff on a weekend to see her. We didn't actually 'finish' we just stopped seeing each other. And I assumed she would find someone else to go out with (well I certainly did not expect her to do nothing in the evenings). This quiet end to our relationship was fine with me because I did not think she was my type for marriage. And she apparently was happy to let it finish.

Well when I moved to Swansea in September 1974 I considered myself to be in a similar situation to when I was going with Miss N. Now it was Miss D, and again I did not think she was my type for marriage (obviously), and, as before, there were no long term plans in place. And I assumed she would find someone else to go out with in the evenings, and finish with me. But it didn't happen this time, because Gx1 wanted to use her to stop me at Swansea university, so he made sure she didn't finish with me (she probably was going out with other blokes in the evening, and she had her 'brother relationship' to keep her busy).

Anyway when I was stopped at Swansea, and pushed back to Cardiff, by Group X as far as I was concerned, I considered myself to be in a disastrous position. I had a 'failed' label attached to me and

Group X quite obviously wanted me to get married to Miss D when I didn't want to know her.

Gx1 Stops My Rugby at the Start of the 1975/76 Season

About four days after my leaving Swansea in September 1975 Gx1 received another shock. I had returned to Cardiff (to live at my parents house) and I went to see an admissions lecturer at Cardiff university (UCC). He accepted me onto a full time course. He considered my 'failure' at Swansea to be not relevant to the course I was starting. This was a disaster for Gx1.

The colleges rugby season had started and for the second game of the season I was in the university's first team. Gx1 had not had time to make covert arrangements to block my rugby at the university (which is what he did at UCS) hence, left to myself and the university rugby lads, I was selected for the first team.

Gx1 immediately moved in with his dirt activities. In the game he got a hit man to fire a laser or electron beam into my chest. This resulted in my going to the infirmary in Cardiff, where I was told I should not play rugby for three months. Gx1 had stopped my Cardiff university first team rugby.

But I was still at the university, going to lectures, what was he going to do about that? It was about three weeks after starting at the university when the lecturer who admitted me to the course told me that someone had objected to my being at the university. This was Gx1, he had got someone, probably one of the people at Swansea university who had been involved in stopping me there, to make the objection. However a few days later my admissions lecturer told me that the objection had been thrown out. So I continued on the course.

For Gx1 it was not going to end there. He wanted me out, failed.

Connections to Earlier Years

In November 1975 Miss D told me that I was invited, with her, to a dinner-dance in Cardiff. Her godfather (in Group X) had made the invite. He owned a business in Newport that was connected to some other businesses in South Wales and it was their annual dinner-dance. We went to the 1973 one, but the November 1974 one I knew nothing about (I was in Swansea).

Whilst dancing with Miss D (stand apart dancing) her godfather walked up to me, and, without saying a word, touched my nose with his hand. We stopped dancing and I looked at him, he just stood there looking at me. After perhaps eight seconds he walked away. I did nothing and started dancing again with Miss D.

When I was driving Miss D home at the end of the night I told her that I was disgusted with what her godfather had done. I didn't think of it as an assault but that is exactly what it was. Perhaps he expected me to say something to him, or hit him, but, as I say, I looked at him and said nothing. So what had caused him to do this? I've discussed this question in early editions of TCF. What I will do here is add a few more details.

Mr Q had got me introduced to the daughter of the secretary of the Welsh Rugby Union (Miss K) soon after I started at UCS in September 1974. He thought that if I started a relationship with her it would mean my playing for Swansea rugby club. He was unaware of Gx1's covert 'fix him, stop him at UCS' activities. Well by the time the early months of 1975 arrived it was apparent that a Miss K and me relationship was about to start.

I'd last seen Miss D's godfather, prior to this November 1975 dinner-dance, in about March 1975. I was at Miss D's place, he appeared for a couple of minutes then left. We said nothing to each other and I remember that he gave me what I would call a dirty look. I'd say he had been told that my relationship with Miss D could soon end, I'd finish with her to go with Miss K in Swansea, and he didn't like it. He, and Gx1, had got me started with Miss D in September 1973 using the, 'innocent church going, living at home, seventeen year old girl, who must be a virgin' stuff. If I finished with her it would be an insult to her, and him, and her parents. 'How dare he turn down such a wonderful girl!' And, even with an understandable, decent, reason for finishing (to go with someone else), it would perhaps be trouble for me.

Did her godfather know about her secret sex with her brother? I'd say, in common with her mother and Gx1, yes. But that was all under heavy wraps. What mattered was the up front 'innocent church girl' public image of Miss D, which would be damaged if I finished with her.

So in March 1975 a test was arranged to see what I thought of Miss D. Details on this are in TCF25, the "note on the windscreen", page 151. This test illustrated that I was not very interested in Miss D. But Gx1 got the result of the test ignored. And he arranged for Miss K's interest in me to end (by getting me poisoned at the meeting that took place prior to a Swansea rugby club game). He wanted me stopped at Swansea university and keeping my relationship with Miss D going, and stopping Miss K, would help him to get what he wanted.

So, surprise, surprise, I was stopped at Swansea in September 1975 and brought back to Cardiff for Miss D purposes (to marry her as far as Gx1 and her godfather were concerned).

But within days of returning to Cardiff Gx1 got a shock, somehow I had managed to continue my university study by starting a course at Cardiff university. The first thing he did was to get a hit man to fire an electron/laser beam into my chest to stop my rugby. I was out of the game for three months.

Then two months after starting at Cardiff university we get to this November 1975 dinner-dance. Here Gx1 inserted the words, 'I'm going to get you'. He didn't make Miss D's godfather say these words, he inserted them in a sort of covert way. The touch on my nose, the assault, was the starter for the words. What this meant was that I was going to be hit. The 'hit' taking the form of hitting me off the Cardiff university course. But then, after that had been done (I was stopped in September 1976), were these hit words rolled on to 1977?

I have said in the past that Gx1 arranged to have me killed in 1977 (using poison on the cross country walk) because he was worried that some Cardiff university lecturers, who had objected to my being stopped, could cause problems for him (my accidental/natural death would end the problems because I wouldn't be around to return to a UCC course). And that stays true today. But it could be that it was at the 1975 dinner-dance when he renewed the idea of killing me, literally (he first tried to do this in 1967), and his, 'I'm going to get you' words, meant, 'I'm going to get you off the UCC course, and, after that I will kill you'.

The source of this affair, Gx1's vile activities, goes back to the 1940s. In "The Knife in the Trunk" chapter earlier in this book I said that Gx1 could have tried to have my father killed by getting malaria to do the job, i.e. arranged for him to be sent on the non day return train journey.

When my father told me about the malaria he got when he was in India in 1945 he told me the name of the place that he was sent to, where he picked it up (he slept rough that night in an empty, parked up, railway carriage). The place was Ranchi.

Within a few months of my starting my relationship with Miss D her godfather moved into a house (a large bungalow) about a mile from Miss D's parents flat. He named the place "The Ranch". The land in front of it was about 20 x 20 yards.

Gx1 probably got him to move to the house, but whether he did or not is unimportant because what matters here is that he certainly got him to name it (I think the godfather was an ex-policeman). The naming of the house tells me two things:

(i) that Gx1 knew about Ranchi, which indicates that he arranged the train journey to try to kill my father, and

(ii) that Miss D was my 'malaria', i.e. he was using her to kill me, either literally, or metaphorically by shipping me to Australia one way, with her as my wife (I would be 'dead' in this country).

Using her to literally kill me could have been done by, at some stage in the relationship, perhaps after I married her, by making sure that I found out about her secret sex with her brother, with the result that I would be killed/murdered to stop me telling anyone else about it.

Someone says, 'okay her godfather wanted you to marry Miss D, why then did he assault you when that could only put you off marriage?' Well Gx1 had got me back to Cardiff, and yes the godfather was happy with that, but then within days I started at Cardiff university. This was a disaster for Gx1 with his 'no degrees for commies' way of thinking. And he immediately went to work on stopping me at the university.

And it was a disaster for the godfather. Me on a three year full time degree course meant marriage was out for three years (no job, no money). And he did not want her to wait that long for marriage. In effect I had pushed Miss D aside and placed education in the priority position. It certainly looked like I was not particularly interested in her. Hence he assaulted me, he probably thought the relationship wouldn't last much longer anyway and that the assault wouldn't make much difference to the situation.

Some weeks later, at the start of January, I finished my relationship with Miss D. I just told her we did not get on with each other.

A bit more on the touch of my nose. It was a 'I'm going to get you' sign by reason of it's connection to India. About twelve months after the malaria there was the knife in the trunk. Which 'said' that the knife was going into my father at a later date. Another name for nose is trunk. Gx1, who told the godfather to touch my nose, my trunk, was 'saying' that he was going to put the knife into me.

Months later I was failed, stopped, at UCC. I had been 'knifed' by Gx1.

The trunk, nose, connection was also used by Gx1 in 1951/52 to 'say' that he was putting the knife into my brother (see page 169 in this book, and TCF25, page 201).

As a rough estimate I'd say this was the twenty second time that Gx1 had used his position to 'put the knife in' to me. And twice, in 1967/8, the 'knife in' was an attempt to kill me, literally.

Good Progress on the Course

By the end of December 1975 it was apparent that my studies at Cardiff university (UCC) were going well. I was getting good or very good marks for essays I done in the subjects. This meant that it looked like I'd have no trouble with the end of academic year examinations and I would be going on to the second year of the course in October 1976.

Gx1 had been told about my progress and for him it was bad news. It meant he would have to arrange new ways to dirty me, to stop me, and from January 1976 on he was very active in this area.

The Gx1 Taxi Poisoning

A week or two into February 1976 I started a part-time taxi driving job on two or three evenings a week.

One evening, a couple of weeks after I started the job, I was told to go to a pub about two miles from the city centre to pick up a fare who would be in a small bar at the side of the pub. It was about 6pm.

The bar was empty apart from one bloke sitting on a stool at the bar. He had a full pint and he asked me if he could buy me a drink while I waited for him to finish his. I said yes to a half pint of shandy. And I sat on a stool alongside him.

In a few minutes we left the bar and I drove him to a housing area a couple of miles away where he paid me, got out of the car and walked off down a side street that joined the road I was on.

The next morning I awoke ill. I was too ill to go into the college and I stayed in bed. It was flu like symptoms, headache, weakness, temperature up.

I felt sure that Group X had got me poisoned.

I had known since September 1975 that Group X were having a go at me (when they got me stopped at Swansea university), and I knew that, with my now being on the Cardiff university course, that they would like to get me stopped again. However I thought they would not be able to interfere (tell college staff what to do) on this Cardiff course. But that wouldn't stop them from hitting me externally, outside the college. And here was one of their external hits.

I stayed in bed for perhaps a week. I did not call a doctor, which seems a bit odd. The only way I can explain this is to say that I never went to a doctor because my health was excellent. I thought that with some over the counter tablets I could get rid of it in a few days.

Yes I was sure I had been deliberately poisoned. A few details told me that. The bloke was on his own with a full pint, which gave him a reason to buy me a drink. It would have been easy for the him to pass his hand over my glass and drop the poison in.

He walked off down a side street. He made sure he did not go into a house while I was around.

I did not report it to the police, well I thought they would never find him. And besides I knew that Group X were in high level positions.

In later years I realised that the barman, who was on his own, could have put the stuff in my glass before filling it. And the police could have questioned him.

Also in later years I noticed a Gx1 'sign' that he had placed into this poisoning. The name of the pub was closely related to the knife that had gone into my father in 1973 (the Gx1 plan to murder him, that was being made to look like an accident, natural causes). The 'sign' was to say that the person who had knifed my father, Gx1, was now 'knifing' me.

The 66 Book

I was in a weekly tutorial for one of the subjects I was doing at UCC. A tutorial is where a small number of students who were doing the subject met in a room to discuss the recent lecture on the subject. There were about six people in the room. The tutorial was chaired by a post graduate student.

The postgraduate student set some homework, we were to read one of two books and do an essay on it. One of the books was titled, 'Zen and the Art of Motorcycle Maintenance'. I was surprised, what did motorcycle maintenance have to do with the subject (which was the Social Structure of Modern Britain). Anyway I ignored the book and did the essay on the other one.

I have never read the book but I know what it is about because years ago I saw it mentioned in the press. It's about a motorbike journey made from one side of the USA to the other. Most of it being on Route 66. Well, well, another 66.

When writing TCF some years back I looked up more details on the book. It was published in 1974 and for some reason it sold quite well. Gx1 had obviously got to hear of it. And for him it was another 66 sign that he could use. Using his influence, he got the book fed into UCC and placed into this tutorial. To say, in his covert language, that it was 66 for me, and out of UCC.

Miss D was 66 (she lived in one). As I have said elsewhere he was using her to get me stopped at UCC (like he did at UCS). He was telling the college, 'he has done a terrible thing by finishing with her, she is a young innocent church going girl, and he should marry her, stopping his study will put him on the right track, push him back to her'.

Gx1 knew all about Miss D. He knew that the 'innocent' young girl bit was rubbish.

Unemployment is Going Up

When I finished with Miss D near the beginning of January this year (1976). I done it over the phone. I just said that our relationship was at an end. Adding that we didn't get on with each other, i.e. I gave no other reason for finishing. She said nothing. In other words we had finished but we were not on bad terms.

In May 1976, before the end of academic year examinations had started at UCC, I met her by accident. One lunchtime I had walked into town, only about 600 yards from the college, and I was just starting my walk back when I met Miss D. She said she had a new car and that it was parked nearby and she would give me a lift to where I was going. I said okay even though I wasn't going far.

The car was a few years old but in good condition. As I got out of the car after the short journey she was saying 'the unemployment figures are going up'. Words I considered to be odd, what did that have to do with her or me?

This meeting was arranged by Gx1. Perhaps he had been told I had headed into town on a fine day and he got her in place ready for my return. Why did he do this? It was because he still had me lined up for her. She was a female that could be shipped out, when married to me, and that is what he was still aiming for, shipping me, with her, to Australia. It was coupled of course to his getting me stopped/failed at the university (for the second time in two years). I would then, he thought, restart my relationship with her (on the basis that it was better to go with her than do nothing).

Perhaps he got her mother to tell her to say, 'the unemployment figures are going up', as I got out of the car. He done this because he knew, in these pre-exam weeks, that I was going to be failed, i.e. 'you will soon be unemployed'.

For a few months now he had been feeding smears/dirt into the college. Presumably he thought they had done the job.

The False Examination Results

The end of academic year examinations arrived in May/June 1976. There were seven three hour examinations. I had no real trouble with any of them. The results came out a week or two later. I was failed in three and passed in four. I was astonished at the results. The three I failed I had found easy, and one of them was my best subject.

For the answer to what happened here first look at Gx1 and his dirt activities. We know that for various reasons he wanted my university study stopped. At the beginning of my UCC course, nine months earlier, he got a hit man to fire an electron/laser beam into my chest to stop me playing rugby for the college. And in recent months he had used his position to covertly smear me, by feeding bits of warped information into the college. The result was that in June the college gave me three fail exam marks. They had been deceived and pressurised into doing it.

What this meant was that I had three re-sit exams to do in September, and I had to pass them then to be able to proceed on the course.

Some of my lecturers were unhappy about this. They knew I had done well in the exams, let's say passed all seven of them, and they thought I should be given the pass marks and proceed to the next year.

But the lecturers didn't have the final say and they were told, perhaps by the registrar, that I had to be given fail results because it looked like I was not going to be allowed to proceed to the next year.

A bit more detail on exam marks. A fail was below

40%, in other words I was expected to believe, in the results that were given to me in June, that I had got a below 40% mark in each of the three subjects when I knew that I was in the 50% to 80% area in each of them.

I had sat many exams over the years and I was never far out in my opinion on how I had done at the end of each examination. If I thought it was easy the result was a pass.

In September I sat the three exams again. And was given fail results. I was again astonished at the results. It meant I could not continue on the course and would have to sign on as unemployed (which is exactly what Gx1 had 'said' in my May meeting with Miss D).

Have you noticed that there is another 37 here. It could be that Gx1, having been told there were seven subjects, seven exams, on my course, told the registrar to make it three fails so as to create one of his signs. He had used 37 before to 'say' that he was going to knife my father in the back in 73, 1973. So 37 'said' that the person who knifed my father, Gx1, was now knifing me.

My lecturers then said, 'well make the fails in his best subjects so that he will have no difficulty with the re-sit exams'.

My Sailing Dinghy's Mast is Broken
by Gx1

It was toward the end of June 1976. I had recently sat the end of academic year examinations at Cardiff university. I decided I'd try dinghy sailing at their sailing club on a reservoir in Cardiff. I liked it and within a week or so bought a second hand sailing dinghy using money I had left over from my grant.

It seems that it was a lecturer at the university that got me to buy it, thinking that, when I placed it at the reservoir, it would help to keep me at the university (he presumably knew that efforts were being made by someone to get me stopped at the university).

I took the dinghy to a river/estuary in west Wales where I stayed for about six weeks.

In west Wales I could increase my sailing skills, which were already adequate. And then when September arrived, when I was due to take three re-sit examinations, I would return to Cardiff and put the dinghy on the reservoir used by the sailing club.

Gx1 knew what the dinghy was about. Knew that it was a 'keep him at the university' purchase. So what did he do? He put the dinghy out of action by getting a hit man to make sure that the mast broke the first time I sailed it. This took place the day after I arrived in west Wales. Details in TCF25, in the section that starts on page 185.

He then made sure that when I ordered a new mast (I had insured the dinghy) it took me till September/October 1977 to obtain it (to ensure the dinghy was not put on the university reservoir during the time when there was a chance I would re-commence at the college).

Here is another thing that occurred during this stay in west Wales. For perhaps three weeks I worked on a farm and the farmer had a son about my age.

One evening the farmer's son got me to go to a pub, with some friends of his, where a dance was being held. He introduced me to a girl and I danced with her for a while. She told me her name. I was surprised to hear that it was the same as Miss D (first name). She was uneasy talking to me, but I couldn't figure out why. After a while we parted and I never saw her again.

Here again is Gx1. He knew where I was and this was a way of pushing Miss D in front of me. When I got back to Cardiff he had a fail ready for me with a push to Miss D. He gave the farmer the instructions and he then told his son what to do. The farmer's son told the girl to tell me her name was --- (Miss D's first name).

This was the only time I went out with the farmer's son. I lived a very quiet life in the weeks I was in west Wales.

The Re-sit Examinations

The September 1976 re-sit exams arrived (three of them), and, as indicated, I had no problems with them. The results came out and they were the same as in the summer, fails (I think it was two fails this time, but it made no difference to the fact that I had to pass all seven subjects to continue the course).

I once again was astonished. I did not believe the results. As far as I was concerned Group X had covertly used their influence to have me stopped by getting false fail results given to me. I had nothing to prove that they had got me stopped so I said nothing about them when I went to see some of my lecturers to express my astonishment at the fails.

So I became unemployed (signed on) and within a week or so I was doing a part time job as a taxi driver. I considered the situation I was in to be ridiculous. I had passed the examinations and so I should have been studying at Cardiff university and playing rugby for their first team.

The Rusty Knife Sign

It was probably toward the end of 1976 when Gx1, using his influence, got me to join a book club.

The club sent me a very low price book every month with details of other books they had on sale that were at a normal price.

Two very low price books they sent me were, "Arigo, the Surgeon with the Rusty Knife", and "Dr Frigo". I kept them.

In 1979/80, when I realised that my father had been hit by Gx1 in 1973, I interpreted the books to mean, "the diagnosis of cancer that wasn't", i.e. the surgeon with the rusty knife. And, "the person who was to give the kill poison to my father at a later date", i.e. Dr Frigo/refrigerator.

The books were Gx1 signs, they 'advertised' what he had done to my father in 1973 and was going to do to him. The rusty/dirty knife part was the small operation my father had first, the operation that gave a false diagnosis of cancer, it was followed a week later by a second operation to remove the so called 'cancerous' area.

That is how I interpreted the books in 1979/80, and it remains valid today (2023). It is possible however that Gx1, whilst being aware of the books connection to 1973, had a second sign in mind for the books.

In the next chapter I tell you about my being poisoned in 1977 by a surgeon. It was an attempt to kill me. This means that Gx1 could have been 'saying', with these books, that a 'rusty knife' would soon be going into me.

The Gx1 Attempt to Murder Me in 1977 on a Cross Country Walk

Over the years Gx1 had spent a lot of time in his office making arrangements to hit me, keep me down. After a hit I got up, and proceeded to once again do well, his response was to hit me, put me down, again. This process had been repeated many times. This hit routine took place in my education, my rugby, my work, and in my relationships with females.

By the time 1977 arrived he could see that his 1976 Cardiff university hit could backfire on him. He had arranged for me to be stopped at the university using false fail results and some of my lecturers didn't like it, and they wanted something done about it.

You could say that he was thinking that I had caused him a lot of trouble over the years, and with it looking like he would have to think up more fix it plans he decided that the best thing to do was to kill me (by 'accident').

Bear in mind that, as well as the Cardiff university false results, he also knew he had arranged the forgery at Swansea university in 1975 and a false cancer diagnosis at the UHW in 1973. So he was getting worried about troublesome Cardiff university lecturers. If they got the false results looked at closely it could uncover his involvement, and that could uncover his other activities.

The murder was to take place in about May 1977 on a long distance cross country walk that Gx1 had arranged specially for the purpose.

Mr G, a friend of mine, worked at the UHW, I had met him in 1973 when I was working there, we sometimes went on training runs together. He got me to go on the walk. It was a walk with a midway checkpoint and everyone could take their own route (using maps) to get there. Mr G introduced me to Mr Z and the three of us, forming our own group, proceeded to the checkpoint.

In the course of the walk I was poisoned by Mr Z. He was a surgeon at the UHW.

It was a death by brain haemorrhage poison. It was meant to result in my being laid out flat, dead, in the country somewhere. The poison however never completed it's job. I had a headache for twenty minutes and for five minutes of this it was agonising. But, evidently, it never burst any blood vessels. When the headache left me I was okay.

At the time the word poison never entered my thoughts. Yes I knew that Group X (Gx1) had got me stopped at Swansea and Cardiff universities, that they were out to keep me down in other words, but poisoning me, killing me, no, I never considered that angle.

It could be that Mr Z was a police surgeon. A position that is generally understood (years ago anyway) to be a surgeon who operates on policemen who are seriously injured in the course of their employment. It follows that Gx1, being a high level police/MI5 official got him to give me the poison. A police surgeon probably does what he is told with no questions asked. If he did ask questions Gx1 would have said nothing about the fact that my death would help to ensure that a number of his dirt activities would stay under wraps (covered up).

It was sometime in 1982 that I realised that what had happened on this 1977 cross country walk was an attempt to murder me.

The details on the walk poisoning can be seen in TCF25, pages 105/7.

The Gx1 Cut Strap

It was September/October 1977 when I received the new mast for my sailing dinghy. I fitted it into the dinghy and then got the rigging/shrouds made to support it.

It was a cold grey morning (probably November) when I took the sailing dinghy with Mr G to Llandegfedd reservoir (twenty miles north east of Cardiff). It didn't occur to me to take it to the reservoir in Cardiff that was used by the university sailing club because by this time university had, for me, finished.

We got the dinghy off the trailer and onto the water. For a couple of minutes we sailed quietly alongside a headland that kept the wind down. When we reached the end of the headland the wind picked up and it was necessary for me to put my feet under the footstrap that was fixed to the bottom of the boat. So that I could lean back, out of the boat, to balance the force of the wind on the sail.

As soon as I took my first lean back the footstrap broke. This meant I went backwards into the water and the wind immediately blew the sail flat onto the water. It then took about ten seconds for the boat to complete the capsize, i.e. the hull uppermost.

We were wearing buoyancy jackets so no problem there. I climbed onto the hull and eventually got the dinghy righted with both of us in it. A small boat with an outboard motor appeared and towed us in.

That night in bed I was thinking about what had happened. The footstrap broke? But how could it have broken when in recent months I had fitted a new footstrap, and made a good job of it to. The strap was woven polyester with a metal plate at each end with screws going through the plates into the hull. I had melted the ends of the strap, which meant they were hard and there was no way the weaving could unravel.

The dinghy was in the garage at the back of the house (I was living at my parents house). The next morning I was in the garage having a close look at the strap. One end of it, the end that had broken away, had a straight clean cut right across it.

There was no doubt about it, someone had, in the days before I took it to Llandegfedd, cut the strap, i.e. someone had wanted me to capsize.

The details are necessary for you to understand this. As I have said the strap was held at each end by a metal plate that was screwed to the boat. The screws went through the plates and the strap. Well what this person did was to use a sharp blade, such as is in a Stanley knife, to cut across the strap right alongside one of the metal plates. He then loosened the plate by unscrewing it's two fixing screws a few turns, and then pushed the cut end of the strap under the plate and up against the screws, and he finished by tightening the screws.

The result was that even if I looked at the strap prior to my using it I would not have seen anything untoward.

The cut end of the strap, as soon as I made my made my first lean back, pulled out from under the metal plate. A force of only a few pounds would have done this because the screws were not going through the strap.

So who done it,? Well I didn't know and left it at that.

You could say, 'Group X had been having a go at you for years, I mean you knew they had got you stopped at Swansea and Cardiff universities, why did you not think they had got the footstrap cut?'

It was because I thought they had finished having

a go at me. I mean they had got what they wanted, me failed/stopped at two universities, so why would they now be messing about with my sailing dinghy?

Writing as of today it is of course obvious that this was Gx1 continuing to use his position to have a go at me. Via a hit man (the person who actually does the job).

So why did he do it? I have said in TCF25, pages 115/19, that he could have had ideas on killing me here (and I explain how he could have arranged it). Well he definitely tried to murder me a few months previous to this, on the cross country walk. That failed so he tried again here. Perhaps, perhaps not. It could be that he just wanted to dirty me, tell some people that I didn't have the ability to sail a dinghy. He would say, 'in west Wales the dinghy capsized the first time he used it and he didn't sail again till recently when he again capsized'. Saying nothing of course about his getting hit men to break the mast in west Wales and cut the strap.

The Letter to the Registrar

The next nine chapters, from here up to the end of the "Official Confirmation" chapter, contain details of my attempts to get the situation straightened out. The "situation" was only the false examination results to begin with, but then, as you will see as you read on, the forgery was added to it, and then the Gx1 plan to murder my father was added to it.

I won't go into what happened to me and Cardiff university in 1977. Nothing much basically. It's what happened in August 1978 that is significant.

It was at this time that I wrote to the registrar of the university saying that I believed my 1976 examination results had been manipulated. I was sure I had passed the three subjects I had been failed in, i.e. that I had been given false fail results. He replied saying that the situation would stay as it was (no comment on my manipulation remark). I continued my efforts to correct things by writing to various people.

I Start a Welsh Office Job

Information on my dispute with Cardiff university (UCC) had evidently reached the Welsh Office. It reached the Welsh Office because the university had said I was correct and they wanted to know how to proceed.

In January 1979 I started a temporary clerical Welsh Office job that had been given to me by the Jobcentre. I was interviewed at the Welsh Office by a woman who had a surname that connected to the word surgeon. This was to 'say' that the Welsh Office had been told about what had been done to my father (by a surgeon at the UHW), had, in other words, been told about the Gx1 plan to murder him. Her name was Mrs Lovett. "Vet" gives veterinary which then gives surgeon.

Yes, when I met her I took note of the vet in her name and that it indicated surgeon. This tells you that by this time, 1979, I had realised that Group X had also hit my father in 1973 (as well as their hitting me at Swansea and Cardiff universities). It all figured, the three went together (like 2 and 2 make 4).

I never really believed my father had cancer in the first place when I was told about it at the UHW in 1973, but I just had to accept it. Well by 1979 I felt sure Group X had arranged with someone in the UHW to give my father a false cancer diagnosis. Why would they do this? Well because they wanted to kill him of course. A diagnosis of cancer meant they could kill him at any time using poison with no questions asked.

I had no thoughts on reporting the false cancer

diagnosis to the police because to start with I had no evidence and anyway Group X were obviously in high level positions.

As I have said elsewhere Group X were, for me in the 1975/79 years, three or four people who sort of acted together. It wasn't until perhaps mid-1979 that I realised that Gx1 was the main problem, where the dirt was. Again I had no thoughts on reporting him to the police. The authorities, the Welsh Office, had obviously started to look into what had been going on over the years and I would leave it to them to sort it out.

The office I was sent to work in was located in town. It was their office for disabled people. What this meant to me at the time was that the Welsh Office had disabled/blocked the Group X plan to murder my father.

This was early days for the Welsh Office. What I mean is yes they had found out about some of what Gx1 had done but there were many of his covert dirt activities that they knew nothing about. By about 1983 I think they had a lot more information on what had been going on over the years.

University Regulations

In February 1979 I decided to try to resolve the UCC dispute by using civil court proceedings. I went to a firm of solicitors. They obtained 'legal advice' and in April told me there was nothing they could do about it.

In October 1979 a university professor in London told me that the Queen was the adjudicator for disputes in welsh universities (stated in university regulations). I replied asking him to send details to her.

After more correspondence the professor, in April 1980, sent me a document containing details of the dispute, adding that I could send it to the clerk of the Privy Council. I did this.

I had some correspondence with the clerk and then in September 1980 he told me the Queen could not, or would not, adjudicate the dispute. I considered this to be very odd.

In "Minus One is Forgery" I told you that the firm of solicitors I went to, as mentioned above, was called "Phillips and Buck". I'd say, without any doubt at all, that the firm was specially named, ready for my arrival. I will explain.

The name of the firm connects to the Queen, because she was living at Buckingham Palace. And the name of her husband was Phillip. In other words the name of the firm was to 'advertise' that any advice they gave me originated from the Queen. This 'connection' indicates that the Queen had already been told about the dispute, in advance of being officially brought into it (named) six months later.

Another interpretation of the firm's name is to say that any advice they gave me originated from Gx1. On the basis that his initials, PTJ, can be seen in the initials of the firm, PAB (there is a T in the A and a J in the B). The name of Gx1's wife was Queenie which supports this interpretation.

It could be that the Welsh Office, who wanted the UCC dispute resolved in my favour, were pushing for me to see a solicitor, and somehow I got directed to this one.

The Constituency Boundary

I will quote two paragraphs from TCF25, page 132.

"In early 1979 I was reading the local evening newspaper when I was surprised to see that our house was involved in a boundary change that would soon be made to some MPs constituencies in Cardiff. The house was on the edge of one constituency and when the change took place it would be in another constituency. I wondered if the change had anything to do with what was going on at Cardiff university (I had written to the registrar of the college in August 1978 about what had happened when I was at the college and the problem was unresolved).

Constituency boundary changes are rare occurrences, they usually go unchanged for decades. A boundary change affecting where I lived a few months after my letter to UCC?"

The boundary change was implemented in the May 1979 general election.

The Job in the Prime Minister's Constituency

In September 1979 it was made known to me that there was a job going selling life insurance policies to students in South Wales. The employer was an insurance broker with his office in Mrs Thatcher's constituency in north London. She was the Prime Minister.

I had an interview at the broker's office and got the job. I made a trip to the office once a fortnight.

I sold quite a few policies. I left the job in about April 1980 to go to a company in Cardiff that sold financial plans. But I never actually started the job.

Two Odd Occurrences in 1979/80

At the end of December 1979, whilst staying at a hotel, I became ill (two days later I was okay).

In October 1980 I was at a seated public meeting in Swansea town hall (Swansea became a city some years on from here). The meeting had nothing to do with what had happened at UCS and UCC. The chairman asked me to expand on a question I had put to the panel that was seated on the stage.

I stood up to do this when all of a sudden there was a loud continuous sound in my ears, it stunned me. I collapsed back onto my seat. It lasted for about thirty seconds. During this time I could hear nothing but the sound and I was incapable of saying anything. When the sound ceased my normal senses returned to me, i.e. I could hear and speak.

In 1979/80 I didn't make anything of these two occurrences. My being ill was surprising when my health was excellent, and what had happened at the meeting was extraordinary, I could not understand what had happened.

It was 1994 when I obtained information that explained these two occurrences. See the chapter later in this book, "The Government Planted False Evidence in 1980". And for a more detailed description of what happened see the chapter of the same name in TCF25.

Civil Court Proceedings

When I went to the solicitors in February 1979 I was thinking that I could use court proceedings to try to resolve the false results situation at Cardiff university. But, as I said, they wouldn't start any proceedings.

By 1981 I had decided to start a claim for damages doing the paperwork myself. Two of the subjects I had studied at Cardiff were in law.

In the claim I also included what had happened at Swansea university. It was a claim for damages from the University of Wales. I cited negligence at Swansea university and breach of contract/fraud at Cardiff university.

At one of the pre-trial hearings (to decide a small issue), it was probably February 1982, I noticed that members of the local press were stood outside the court. I asked the judge if they could come into the court, and hence report on the proceedings. He said they could not. This, it seems, is when the censorship of this affair started.

In April 1982 my claim against the UW was struck out, cancelled by the court. Soon after this I gave details of what had happened in the 1970s to the police.

By about the end of 1982 the authorities had gathered more information on the activities of Gx1 and placed him in the dirt category.

1983, Forgery, Not a Mistake

In January 1983, having suspected it for sometime, I became sure, as a result of enquiries I had made, that I had been given fixed question papers in the Pure Mathematics end of academic year examination at Swansea university in 1975 (a two part exam, i.e. two three hour exams). In the first examination the incorrect question paper had not been given to all the examination candidates (a mistake). Only I had been given a fixed question paper. The others had been given the correct question paper. Then in the second examination it was repeated (I was again given a fixed question paper, to match the one I had been given in the first exam). I updated the police with this information.

I was calling the question papers "fixed" question papers. By July I had formed the opinion that they were forged documents. Details on how I formed this opinion are in TCF6, page 65, and TCF9, page 69.

In September I sent the police copies of the forged question papers I had been given (I still had the originals). They investigated. They did not confirm the forgery, they said they had been told that all the examination candidates had been given the incorrect question paper in the first examination, then an adjusted question paper in the second examination. This was the 1975 version of events, as given to me in 1975 by the lecturer who invigilated the first examination. It was a cover up story, and the police had accepted it.

I sent the police evidence that supported what I

said had happened. This included statements and an affidavit from people who had sat the examination. But they would do no more.

The Prime Minister is Wrong

In February 1985 I delivered the forged (altered) examination question papers I had been given at Swansea university in 1975 to the police headquarters in Bridgend. I had kept all my Swansea and Cardiff university papers (lecture notes, essays etc and examination question papers).

I decided to postpone any more civil court proceedings. As well as my claim against the UW I had started a separate claim against Cardiff university which the court, in pre-trial proceedings in 1984, had struck out, cancelled. I made this postponement decision knowing that in law if an act incurs both civil and criminal liability the criminal part of it is dealt with first. What had happened at both universities was criminal. In other words a prosecution had to be next, with the civil court money claims being resolved after it had finished.

I contacted various people and the media saying that I had given the police evidence that substantiated my accusation of forgery at Swansea university and that contrary to standard procedure a prosecution had not been started. For a while I got no sensible response (the media were censored), then I found an MP who said he would write to the Prime Minister about it. He did and she replied saying "there is no evidence" to show that a criminal offence had been committed. She had apparently based her words on the police investigation of 1983 and their letter to me at the time in which they gave me the investigation results. But after their investigation I had sent them evidence that supported my accusation. She had in other words ignored the fact that the police now, in 1986, had evidence that supported my accusation.

Because the MP wouldn't write to her again I wrote to her and enclosed copies of the evidence I had given to the police. I received a reply, signed by a person in her office, saying she would not do any more.

Official Confirmation

In September 1987 the police acknowledged, in writing, that documents I'd given to them, examination question papers I'd been given at Swansea university in 1975, were forged documents (documents used to deceive and defraud).

They knew gave the documents to me (two members of staff), and they presumably knew who made them.

Having stated that the Swansea question papers were forgeries the police would surely now have to say something about my other accusations.

In November I wrote to the police asking them if they had confirmed that my father had suffered criminal injuries in 1973 (as a result of Group X activities). I first told the police about what had been done to him in July 1985 and in October 1986 I gave them more details. They made no comment. And in their reply to this November letter they again made no comment.

Later in November I wrote to the police again. I said, "has your investigation confirmed that three end of academic year examination results given to me in 1976 at University College Cardiff as fails, were lies/fraudulent?" In their reply they did not answer my question.

Details on the last two paragraphs are in TCF6, page 134.

I had of course assumed a prosecution would start. But this did not happen. And I found myself again contacting various people and the media (who were definitely censored), telling them about the incorrect/absurd legal situation that was now in existence.

No one would do anything of relevance and in 1990 I gave up trying to get the situation straightened out and decided that sometime in the future I'd write a book about it.

The Government Planted
False Evidence in 1980

In the course of 1994 it was made known to me that what had happened at Swansea town hall in October 1980 was a government hit. It was done to plant false evidence into the dispute to ensure that I lost.

Up to October 1980 Cardiff university (UCC) were backing me, they knew I was correct about the 1976 false results. In other words me and the university were on course for winning the dispute, which was proceeding under wraps. Yes I say that "me and the university" would win because they would be able to put their position right. Justifying the false results by saying that Gx1 had deceived/ pressurised them, into doing it.

The government did not want his activities brought into public view because he was a covert MI5 government employee. So they arranged the town hall false evidence plant. It could be that they gave Gx1 the go ahead to arrange it. The purpose of the plant was to deceive the UCC staff who were of course closely following the dispute. UCC, up to this point, considered me to be a perfectly sensible individual.

In the hit my credibility was destroyed, I was made to look stupid, 'he collapses when under pressure'. It was a 'bullet' fired at me by a government hit man that caused me to collapse. The bullet took the form of a directional sound beam directed at my head, my ears (see the chapter "Laser, Electron and Sound Beam Devices" later in this book). So UCC, who were deceived, stopped supporting me. In effect, without them to back me, I had lost the dispute.

You can see details of the town hall hit in TCF25, pages 38 and 40/1.

This information I received in 1994 explained a lot. I now had an answer to the questions:

(i) why, in the 1980s, would many of the people I contacted do nothing?

(ii) why was I getting letters from people that missed the point?

(iii) why wasn't a prosecution started?

A prosecution wasn't started because the people who were running this under wraps dispute (the civil court judge in 1982 then the police and then the Crown Prosecution Service) knew about the false evidence that had been planted by government officials at the town hall in 1980 and they didn't want a civil court judgement or a prosecution to accept the con, i.e. accept the false evidence as genuine evidence. So they ensured that people I contacted about it, in my efforts to get a prosecution started, either done nothing or failed to understand what I was talking about. They presumably thought that the 1980 town hall plant should not have been done in the first place.

A possible alternative to having no corrupted prosecution was for a prosecution to be started and at the beginning of it the government prosecutor would say that the evidence obtained at the town hall in 1980 was false and that it had been planted by government officials. Evidently the government would not authorise this. Or should I say, the people who run this country, would not let this happen.

More on the 1979 Boundary Change

The May 1979 boundary change is mentioned earlier in this book.

I have no doubt in saying that the boundary change was because of my dispute with Cardiff university. The change only involved a small area of land, perhaps one or two hundred houses, why bother to make a small boundary change? The obvious answer is that it was because Gx1 wanted to get our house out of the MP's constituency we were in and into a new constituency with a new, different, MP.

He wanted to do this because he knew the dispute was heading for an MP and that my present, pre-boundary change, MP, had been told by the Welsh Office that I was correct, and that hence he would support me, back me.

By getting a different MP in place (who had not been told by the Welsh Office that I was correct) he could fix things, prepare the MP, to ensure that he didn't back me.

So who was the MP for our house before the boundary change, the one he wanted to avoid? The answer is I don't know. In the months before May 1979 I hadn't thought of contacting my MP which means I hadn't looked up who it was. In more recent years I have looked at the internet to try to get an answer to this question but without success.

In June 1979 I wrote to my MP about the dispute. It was Ian Grist (the boundary change had come into effect in May 1979 at a general election). After some delay he contacted Cardiff university about the dispute. And that was about it. In November he said there was nothing he could do about it.

The general election had taken place about six months before it was due to take place because the pre-election government of Mr Callaghan had become unpopular.

The months before the election were labelled by the media as "the winter of discontent". The discontent being some industrial unrest.

"Winter of discontent" gives w o d, which gives Welsh Office discontent. A coincidence?

Cardiff university and the Welsh Office knew I was correct in saying I had been given false results in 1976 and both of them wanted it shown (in public) that I was correct. With the university explaining that they were deceived and pressurised into stopping me (by giving me the false fail results) by Gx1.

The people who ran this country decided that they were not going to let this happen. Gx1 was a high level government official (probably in MI5) and they wanted to keep anything he had done in the dark.

I am quite sure that the phrase "winter of discontent" was fed into the media by someone who wanted to illustrate, in a covert way, that the Welsh Office were not satisfied with something.

The Welsh Office from say November 1978 (when they received details of the dispute), wanted it forwarded to my MP. The people that ran the country, along with Gx1, decided that my MP wasn't suitable, it looked like he would come out on my side. So they arranged to have my writing to my MP delayed until after they had got their MP in position. And instead of holding things up till after November 1979 when the general election was due to take place, they arranged for the early general election (by creating the industrial unrest) which meant I could write to my (their) MP soon after it took place.

I will point out here that in 1981 I met Michael Roberts in the Welsh Office. He was a Cardiff MP. He appeared to be unhappy with the situation but he would not say anything to me about it. Was he the MP for where I was living pre the May 1979 boundary change?

Sometime later, in 1982, I met Mr Roberts a second time. It was at his house in Cardiff. The meeting only lasted a few minutes, it was obvious he was unhappy about something, but again he wouldn't say anything to me about it.

In February 1983, Mr Roberts, a healthy fifty five year old, died suddenly. He was about to say something in the House of Commons.

More on the Job in the Prime Minister's Constituency

In 1979 the unresolved dispute was placed in front of Mrs Thatcher. Placed not by me but by the people who were handling the dispute. The job I started in her constituency in September of this year was to 'tell me' that it had been sent to her.

Was this the first time the dispute had reached Prime Minister level? It seems the answer is no. It appears that Mr Callaghan, in the position until May 1979, had been told about it. When was he told about it? If he was told about it in the last few months of 1978 it could mean that he helped to create the winter of discontent by making some bad decisions.

I believe Mr Callaghan knew about the dispute because straight after my temporary Welsh Office clerical job finished in March 1979 I went into a temporary clerical job with the Inland Revenue. It appears this was to 'tell me' that the dispute had been forwarded to Mr Callaghan. Why do I say this? Because Mr Callaghan was closely connected to the Inland Revenue. Before he became an MP, which was in 1945, he had spent seven years working in the Inland Revenue and this was followed by five years or so working for an Inland Revenue trade union.

Perhaps Mr Callaghan decided to put the dispute in the pending tray, i.e. he would not give a decision either way on it. And it was to be left to Mrs Thatcher to make the decision.

Anyway the dispute, in the latter part of 1979, was apparently forwarded to Mrs Thatcher. So what happened next?

At the end of December 1979 I was poisoned. Then on the first day of January 1980 I found myself, feeling ill, on the flat roof of a hotel that was about eight stories high. The details are in TCF25, page 37. I won't add any comments now I will instead go straight on to what happened in October 1980 at Swansea town hall.

There is no doubt that at the town hall I was hit by government officials. They planted false evidence into the dispute to ensure that I lost the support of UCC.

So it looks like Mrs Thatcher made the town hall hit decision, gave the go ahead. The alternative was to have a public hearing in which an MI5 employee would be shown to be the cause of my getting stopped at the university. And she would not have that.

I have to add here that the Queen, in 1979/80, who had received details of the dispute, because she was named in university regulations as the adjudicator for disputes in welsh universities, presumably knew about Mrs Thatcher's involvement.

The adjudication that was on offer, according to the university regulations, would have provided a hearing (perhaps in public) that would enable Cardiff university to say I was correct about being given false fail results whilst at the same time placing the blame for what had happened on Gx1. Saying that he had used his position to deceive/pressurise them into stopping me.

But, as I have told you, the clerk of the Privy Council told me, in September 1980, that the Queen would not hold an adjudication hearing. Presumably because she would not let an MI5 employee get picked out as being the cause of the false results.

I sum up this chapter by saying, 'who exactly was involved in making the decision to plant false evidence at the town hall?'

The Two Gx1 Attempts to Murder Me in the 1960s

I have said in TCF25 that the 1967 and 1968 Gx1 attempts to murder me (by 'accident') were because he wanted to stop me starting a full time university course in September 1968. The firm I worked at, AEI, and the college I was studying part-time at, Llandaff Tech, had made a decision in 1967 that I should start at university in 1968.

My going to university was of course very much against Gx1 long term plans and thinking. For some years now he had me pencilled in for a one way journey to Australia (to stay with my brother) and anyway university courses for commies were not on (I was a commie in his mind).

So in 1967 he decided to murder me. This would ensure I did not go to university. I wouldn't be around to ship to Australia a few years on from here but that was not important to him. What mattered was his plan to murder my father at the end of the mortgage (in 1973) and he had to make sure nothing got in the way of that.

You could say, 'it was a bit heavy handed for him to go for murder as a way of stopping you going to university'. Yes I would agree. What it indicates is that he was into murdering people, i.e. he'd done it before and so why not here? Consider the fact that in 1969/70 he murdered the carpenter's son. And in 1964 he poisoned Ted Heath when he was in Cardiff. I think this was an attempt to kill him there and then but he survived (as a semi invalid) for a few more years.

I have not given you details of Gx1's attempt to murder me in 1967 (in this book or in TCF25). This is because I cannot give details of it to you, the public. All I can tell you is that he used covert methods to attempt to murder me. And he was very close to getting the job done successfully. As it was I came through it unscathed.

It is possible that the reason Gx1 had for killing me in August 1968 was not to stop me entering university in September 1968. I say this because it appears that he applied some dirt to me in July 1968 and he could have used this to stop me entering university. If this was the case why then did he try to murder me in August 1968?

Well the answer would be to stop my rugby. The rugby season was about to start and I was the captain of the Llandaff Tech team and it looked like I was on course for Cardiff rugby club. One way of stopping this was to kill me. When the August 1968 BD hit turned out to be unsuccessful he, a couple of weeks later, came out with a new way of stopping my rugby, the false hairline fracture of my left ankle.

Gx1 Attempts to Murder a Musician

I have another Gx1 poisoning to tell you about. In 1964 Ted Heath and his band (popular british musicians) had a night playing at a venue in Cardiff. During the course of this he had a brain haemorrhage. He was taken to hospital in Cardiff and a week or two later transferred to his home in London where he had nursing care on a 24 hour basis. He never returned to leading the band and died in 1969.

Why did Gx1 do it? Presumably it was to give a 'sign' that said the poison was going in, and had gone in, at the Heath in Cardiff. My father would be knifed in the hospital located there and perhaps the kill poison was to be given to him at the same time. And the poison, the knife, had been put into me there in the 1960 baseball game.

The poisons used by Gx1 for the carpenter's son, Ted Heath, and me on the cross country walk in 1977, were 'kill by brain haemorrhage' poisons. Was the same poison used for all three of us?

There are many astonishing activities, hits, that I have told you about in this book, TCF25 and earlier editions. All of them were arranged by Gx1, a warped high level british government official. These activities of his took place over a period of thirty six or so years (1945 to 1981).

I think that numerous pages in these books contain details that will shock some people. When writing them I have at times found it necessary to stop writing, get into bed to keep warm, and continue later.

Ages ago I placed a "warped" label on Gx1. Yes but I would say that he could also be labelled a fanatic. Not in the openly vociferous way, he never had much to say, but in his way of thinking, which was obtained from british government anti-commie rhetoric that was first put out in the 1940s. It was part of his job to apply the rhetoric. And the way he did it has to place him in the fanatical idiot category.

The Heath hospital in Cardiff is one reason for why Gx1 arranged to have Ted Heath poisoned, it gave him his sign, his connections. but he could also have had a second reason for doing it.

A few years ago I read a paperback book that had been written by Ted's wife on their life together. In the book she said that on one occasion Ted and his band were invited by the Queen to play at Windsor Castle (one of the Queen's homes). But it never got past the invitation stage because the Queen wanted him to play for nothing. Ted said he would do it if he was paid. No agreement was arrived at and the performance didn't take place.

People may have varying views on this, I would say that for Ted, paying himself and perhaps twenty of his musicians for the performance, was a lot of money. Bear in mind that when he started in the musical business he had often played to the public on the streets of London for pennies. Since those days he had become a successful musician and bought a house (on a mortgage) in London. But I'd say he still had to watch his money.

Gx1 could have considered Ted's response to this Windsor Castle invitation to be an 'affront/ insult' to the Queen. And so he deserved to be hit. As I have said Gx1 was fanatical in his anti-commie activities and he was no doubt just as fanatical in his support of the Queen.

The Year in Swansea

I will go over my year in Swansea here, adding a few things I have not mentioned before.

Up to September 1975 odd occurrences that had taken place in earlier years had, as far as I was concerned, just happened, had happened naturally that is. There was however one exception, it was in 1973 when I first suspected that something odd was going on. The hospital diagnosis given to my father, 'that can't be right', I thought. His work kept him fit, and my mother's food with her numerous home made recipes meant that he was in excellent health. He didn't have an ounce of unnecessary fat on him. But at the time I had nothing to go on and I hadn't formed any group x ideas so I didn't point the finger at anyone.

But September 1975, when I was suddenly stopped at Swansea university, was a different matter. The odd occurrences of three months earlier plus the obvious push to Miss D (back to Cardiff) made me sure that three or four influential people outside of the university (Group X) had fixed things, got me stopped.

One oddity that I noticed when I first went to Swansea was the fact that the lecturer who talked to me about starting at the university said I could only go on the first year of four years. A preliminary year if you like to call it that to the standard three years it takes to get a degree. With a HNC, which I had, I should have gone straight into the first of three years. But he said it was the first of four or nothing so I said yes to it. This is a definite indicator that shows that Gx1 had got in here, telling the college that it was only going to be a one year stay for me (hence they put me on an 'unimportant' preliminary year).

Gx1 knew that my rugby would be a problem for him at the college. For years he had been making sure I did not play in top level rugby. If I played for the college it would be a step toward playing for Swansea rugby club. So he fixed it so that I did not play for the college.

SV, a member of staff at the university, was I think the person who put the Gx1 'stop his rugby' plan into effect. He was the hit man, the person acting on instructions 'from above'. He used covert methods within days of my starting at the college to dirty me with one of the lads that ran the rugby team.

The rugby players knew I had played at the Wasps because I trained in a Wasps jersey (in those days the top teams jerseys could only be obtained by players at the clubs, i.e. they were not on sale in the shops to anyone like they are today). But nevertheless, as I said, as a result of SV's dirt activities, I was kept out of the rugby team, and I wasn't even selected for the second team.

This astonishing fact, a person who was a first team player at the Wasps (would have been if it was not for Gx1 'stop him' activities), one of the top teams in the country, not even being selected for the second team at Swansea university, tells us, on it's own, that something very odd, very wrong, was going on at the college.

A covert indicator that 'says' that Gx1 had arranged to stop me playing for the college is the address that I moved into when I first went to Swansea (after two or three days in a bed and breakfast place). Gx1 selected the street and told the college accommodation office to find me a place in it. For Gx1 the name of the street was a 'sign' that said that my rugby at the college was 'dead'.

The street's name was the first name of the head

of the department at Bart's. It was he, on Gx1 instructions in 1971, that ensured that my playing for the Wasps first team did not happen, it was 'dead'. In other words his name on the street I was living in at Swansea meant that my rugby in Swansea was also 'dead'.

The name of the Bart's head of department gave another 'sign' in 1971. It was 'you to Australia'. My moving from Cardiff to the Bart's job in London in March 1971 was a step toward the one way flight from London that Gx1 had planned for me in 1972. So the street I was living in at Swansea also meant that Gx1 had me pencilled in, again, for a one way ticket to Australia. And that, for him, meant one year and out, because he wasn't going to wait another three years (to get a degree) for the ship out job to take place.

Then we get to the acid that was covertly put on the laces of my rugby boots, to 'say', 'your rugby is dead'. It was almost certainly SV that done this.

Then Gx1, using his covert dirt activities (the 1975 pub poisoning), blocked the possibility of my starting a relationship with the daughter of the secretary of the Welsh Rugby Union, Miss K. She had been put in place by Mr Q who was trying to get things put right for me on the rugby front. Mr Q knew that I had been improperly blocked at the Wasps, i.e. stopped from playing in their first team. If I started a relationship with Miss K it would mean my playing for Swansea rugby club.

And it was at this time that Gx1 inserted the Basey 'sign' into what was going on. Another sign that said 'your rugby is dead', this sign had the word 'forever' attached to it.

And then in April 1975 Gx1 got me into accommodation that was in a street that had Miss D's first name in it (in group x language), i.e. I was on Miss D street. And that meant I would soon see my study at the college stopped and get pushed back to

Cardiff where I would be expected to take Miss D out regularly (she lived near Cardiff) and marry her. In fact I had a very good reason for not wanting to know her.

Gx1 knew all about Miss D, he knew what she was up to, that she was trouble in other words, which is why he got me going out with her in the first place. She followed the pattern of what he'd been doing to me in the past (tried to kill me, etc). What he didn't know was that I had picked up on what she was up to, because I'd said nothing about it to anyone (including Miss D). He thought that with some pushing (getting me out of Swansea and back to Cardiff), he could make me marry her.

Then in the end of academic year examinations I had forged/altered question papers given to me in one of the examinations. To ensure I left the college, failed. Yes SJ and SF gave me the forged papers (it was a two part examination, two three hour exams) but who made them? Was it SJ, or someone else?

I believe SV was around when the first of the two examinations took place, and I'd say it was he that made the forged papers, i.e. he obtained the correct question papers from the mathematics department, altered one of them (the paper for the first examination), and then gave it to SJ, telling him to give it to me in the examination. He then made the paper that was given to me in the second examination 'fit' the paper that was given to me in the first examination.

In each of the two examinations the Forgery Act was broken, and in so doing it gave a 66 'sign'. A sign that meant 'you are going to Miss D' (she lived in a 66), and 'out of Swansea'. Then near the end of my one year in Swansea there was another 66 'sign', this was in a car I was put on to and bought. The car said, 'run fast to Miss D'.

What happened in my year at Swansea is extraordinary. And it is only a part of what Gx1 done to me and my family. In previous years he had hit us

140

many times. And he continued with his covert dirt activities after the Swansea year.

The Secret Sex Relationship

I will summarize my relationship with Miss D and add some things I haven't told you about before.

At the start of my relationship with her I had doubts about the 'innocent church going girl' image that she had put out. She just didn't seem to fit it.

As the weeks went on my doubts about her increased. Six months after starting with her I formed the opinion that she was in a secret sex relationship with her brother, and had been before I started with her.

This of course was lethal, I knew it was a criminal offence. But all I had to go on was small signs that added up to it, meaning that I had no usable proof, and I had no thoughts on reporting them to the police.

One of the "small signs" was the odd "Brotherly Love" occurrence. I have said a bit about it in TCF25, I will go over it again here. It happened about three months after I'd started with Miss D. I called at her place one evening to take her out for a drink. Her mother said we could, instead of going out, go into Miss D's bedroom for a while. This had never happened before.

We went into the bedroom and straightaway I started to look at things in the room, to find something to talk about. On a chest of drawers there was a small bookstand that had about five books on it. I looked at the titles of the books and one of them stood out for me. It did this because it had the title "Brotherly Love". And, with Miss D being religious, in that she went to church every week, I assumed it

142

was a book on religion. So I decided to use the book to get her to talk about her religious ideas.

I showed her the book and asked her about it. She didn't say a word, she had frozen. Very odd. I left it at that and found something else to talk about.

About two weeks later her mother again said we could go into Miss D's bedroom for a while (this was the second and last time we did this). I looked at the books on the bookstand. The Brotherly Love book wasnt there. It was not a library book, which meant that Miss D had removed the book from the bookstand presumably because she didn't want me to refer to it again. I said nothing to her about the missing book, it was just something I noticed.

What happened here helped me, three months later, to form the opinion that she was in a secret sex relationship with her brother (who was in his thirties). For her the book meant 'sex with my brother' and it shocked her into silence when I wanted her to talk about the book.

When I formed my opinion I decided that the thing to do was finish with her. But this was a problem. How was I going to do it when the 'nice innocent church going girl' image that she had put out, and was accepted by various people, meant that if I finished with her, saying nothing about her sex with her brother, I would be placed in the 'bad category'.

It would go like this, 'what a terrible thing to do, finish with an innocent eighteen year old church going living at home girl who must have been a virgin when he started to go out with her'. In other words I thought that if I finished with her, saying nothing, I'd be hit in some way or other (like put me out of a job or get me physically hit).

So a quick finish coupled to saying nothing was out. At least it was most definitely not to be recommended. And, as for accusing her of sex with her brother and then finishing with her, well that would undoubtedly mean trouble for me (because I had no proof).

I decided to go for the quiet, long term, say nothing about it finish. Let the relationship run down in other words in the expectation that she would finish with me, believing that I wasn't interested in her. This way of finishing would leave me in the clear. I wouldn't be hit because I didn't do it.

In September 1974 I moved to Swansea to start a full time course at the university (UCS), and this I thought would finish the relationship, because of course it meant I'd see less of her. She would, hopefully, in her many vacant evenings, find someone else to go out with and finish with me. But this did not happen and Gx1, in March 1975, fed in to the college, 'fail him, it will get him back to Cardiff to marry the innocent church going girl he is going with' (he knew this was rubbish of course). He wanted me stopped because his vile plans did not include me getting a degree. He was lacking some important information. He, like Miss D, did not know that I knew about her secret sex with her brother.

In September 1975 I was stopped at Swansea university and forced back to Cardiff. Three months later I put an end to my relationship with Miss D (I said nothing about her secret sex relationship).

It is worth knowing, though it must be obvious anyway, that I never, at any time in the relationship with Miss D, said 'I love you'. I certainly didn't. I had my doubts about her when I started with her and things had deteriorated from then on.

During sex she was turned off, it was like she done it but wasn't that interested in it. It was her brother who turned her on, he had sex with her from the rear. I found this out in the days before I finished with her.

What I have just said, at the end of the last paragraph, requires more information to enable you to understand it. I gave these details in TCF6, page 257, and TCF9, page 183. What I will do is go over them again here.

It was the end of December 1975 (a month after the dinner-dance assault) when Miss D came to see me on a weekday lunchtime at my parents house (where I was living). Both my parents were out. We proceeded toward sex and I asked her to turn round and bend over a sofa.

In sex I was completely conventional. It was always the standard front to front sex. My asking her to turn round, for sex from the rear, was very unusual, I had never done it like that before. Anyway for some reason I asked her that, she turned round, and we started sex.

She was transformed. She was noisy and excited, which surprised me a lot. Prior to this, with standard front on sex, she was, as I said, always turned off, she done it but it didn't mean much to her.

One word she said during this rear sex was clear, it was her brother's name. This made me pause, I said nothing and continued.

We finished sex. She turned round and held me, she was in a semi-shocked state. I asked her what she had said. She answered with, "nothing". I said nothing and left it at that.

Why did I ask her what she had said when I knew what she had said? Well that's easy for me to answer. I was carrying on with the decision I had made when I first formed the opinion that she was having sex with her brother (say nothing about it because I had no usable proof).

By saying, "what did you say?", I was in effect inviting her to tell me about it. But she wouldn't do that. She believed that I knew nothing about it, and she was going to keep it that way.

Was her saying her brother's name usable proof? Proof that I could give to the police? It's debatable. She could tell them, 'I never said that, he's lying'. My idea of usable proof was a picture of them at it, or a document signed by Miss D saying that she was in a sexual relationship with her brother, and I didn't have either of those. Anyway I did not consider this angle at the time and days later I finished the relationship.

Thinking about Miss D now I realise that I never, ever, saw her laugh. And I don't even recall seeing her smile, quite unbelievable but true. She had a sombre sort of character.

Let's look closer at what would have happened if I had accused her of being in a secret sex relationship with her brother.

(i) if I had done this when I first formed my opinion I definitely do not think she would have said, 'yes that's correct'. She knew I had seen nothing (not seen them at it) and she would have denied it. We would then have been in an argument situation. The relationship could not have continued with such an accusation openly stated and I'd end the relationship.

(ii) if I had done it when I unexpectedly arrived at her place when she and her brother were having sex (July 1974) it would have ended my relationship with her. I didn't actually see them at it and so I said nothing. I 'played thick', with success, they thought I did not realise what they were up to. I was continuing with the decision I had made four months earlier, i.e. say nothing about it because I had no proof. Details on this can be seen in TCF6, pages 250/2 and TCF9, pages 176/8.

(iii) if I had made the accusation straight after the rear sex, i.e. 'you said your brother's name, it's obvious you are having sex with him'. I still think she would have denied it, saying, 'I didn't say that'. And I'd end the relationship.

(iv) if, straight after the rear sex, I had made the accusation and she replied with 'yes I am'. Very unlikely but let's look at it anyway. Well I'd still end the relationship. It now being in the open would have made no difference to the fact that she was a deceiver when she considered it to be necessary. Words that could have come from her like, 'I will stop it', would have meant nothing to me.

146

So whichever way you look at it my accusing her of sex with her brother would have ended the relationship. But then what?

She had a close relationship with her mother and she would tell her why I had finished with her, tell her what I had accused her of. I believe that her mother knew that she was in a sexual relationship with her brother, she got it started in the first place. But did Miss D know that her mother already knew about it? I don't know. Let's assume here that Miss D thought her mother knew nothing about it. Her mother would have taken up the, 'how dare he accuse you of that', attitude (this would have fitted her bent way of thinking).

My finishing with her daughter was in itself an insult to the 'innocent church going girl' image that had so carefully been propagated. 'She's not good enough for you eh! I'll see about that.' But more than that, much more than that, I had accused her of a criminal offence. 'Has he told anyone else about it?', she could have said to her daughter. 'I don't think so', would have been the reply. Her mother could then have decided, with her Group X friend, to get me hit, perhaps killed, before I put it about.

And that is why I decided in the first place (when I formed my opinion) to say nothing about it and go for the quiet, slow, disinterested, finish to the relationship. I knew that if I accused her of sex with her brother (without solid proof) I could find myself in big trouble.

An accusation like that, an accusation that her daughter was a criminal. A daughter who was still living at home, and who was supposedly a seventeen year old virgin when I started to go out with her, and who went to church every week, and played the piano. If the accusation was given to the police and she had been prosecuted her 'church going girl' image would be shattered.

Gx1, before I started the relationship with Miss D, knew about her sex with her brother. He, her godfather, and her mother seemed to be on a sort of covert dirt information grapevine.

Recall the time when Gx1, three months after my starting with Miss D, made it known to me (via his wife) that he had a place for me to live when I got married to her. It was rooms in a house that, on the ground floor, was used as an office that he sometimes worked in (part-time). He wanted to get in on her turned on 'rear, brother, sex'. Which would be a big sex turn on for him. He knew all about it alright.

Earlier in this book I told you that sometime around the end of 1973 Miss D's godfather moved to a house that was about a mile from where she lived (with her parents). He bought an electronic organ (I was at the place once with Miss D and I was shown it). He didn't play it, he bought it so that Miss D could play it (she played the piano). And that is apparently what she did, went there, I don't know how often, to play it.

Can you figure out another reason for why she went there? I'd say her godfather was making use of her turned on 'rear, brother, sex'. In other words he bought the organ to get her there, it gave her a plausible reason for her visits.

A Summary of the Gx1 'Your Rugby is Dead' Activities

In this book and in earlier books on this affair I have detailed the many times that Gx1 hit my rugby. What I will do now is attempt to place these rugby hits in one chapter, this chapter. In a few places I add more detail to what I have said previously (to make things clearer).

I got my initial rugby training, if I can call it that, from my father and the tv. This took place in my aged eight to eleven years when we both watched the international games on tv. For decades rugby had been in our family and my father was keen on the game. He had however stopped going to inter-national and club games some years earlier. Then at the school I started in September 1959, aged eleven, I played my first game of rugby.

I remember the first school mid-week sports day. The physical education teacher was picking the teams for a game of rugby for the eleven to thirteen years of age players. He had perhaps one and a half teams on the pitch which comprised of second year players and he was looking at the new first year players who were standing round hoping to be selected for the game. He called me over and put me on the pitch for the game. And from there on I was always in the mid-week sports day rugby game, and I was also in the school team that played other schools on a Saturday morning.

In more recent years I have formed the opinion that on that first mid-week rugby game day the physical education teacher picked me out from perhaps twenty rugby hopefuls because someone had told him that my brother had played for Cardiff Boys.

At the end of that first season it was stated, in the school end of academic year report, that I was "outstanding" at rugby.

Gx1 was very disturbed by this. "Outstanding" meant that I was on course for Cardiff Boys and Wales Boys. He got to hear of it from the sort of 'covert grapevine' that we have in this society. And he, being in a high level government job, was very much a part of the covert grapevine. For him it was bad news. He had my father pencilled in for death some years on from here (when the mortgage was finished) and a one way 'ship out' plan for me. Significant success for me in rugby in the coming years would cause problems for both these plans.

The 'ship out' plan was me to Australia on a one way ticket a few years on from here to join my brother (twelve years older than me). He had been shipped there in the 1950s by Gx1 and got married there and stayed there.

Within a week or so of the end of this, my first rugby season, Gx1 arranged 'the diamond hit', to dirty me. Put down the physical education teacher's high opinion of me. And a couple of weeks after that he arranged 'the cap over the cemetery wall' occurrence. This was a 'sign', a statement in his covert language, saying that significant success for me in rugby was 'dead', i.e. the Wales Boys cap was in a cemetery.

About two years later he got the physical education teacher moved from our school to a job in another Cardiff school. I did not play for Cardiff Boys.

I stopped playing rugby when I left school and didn't play the game again till the 1967/68 season, when I was nineteen. I was studying one day a week at Llandaff Technical College in Cardiff and they had one rugby team. It played adult fixtures (age nineteen and over) against various teams in the Cardiff area, and I played for them. At the end of the season the players voted me captain for the next season.

I didn't know this at the time but I can now say that the lecturer at the college who arranged the fixtures for our rugby team had plans for my rugby. He thought I should play for Cardiff rugby club. And he lined up a suitable female for me (I wasn't going with anyone). This went into the covert grapevine, which means that Gx1 got to hear of it. And he didn't like it one bit, his covert plans to murder my father and ship me out were again threatened. For him it was, 'stop his rugby'.

In the second game played by the Llandaff Tech rugby team at the start of the 1968/69 season, when I was captain of the team, Gx1 struck. From his high level government job he could arrange activities of all sorts, and these included covert vile activities, that would, under public conditions, be called criminal/corrupt. And here, to stop my rugby, he arranged for me to be given a false hospital diagnosis of a fractured ankle. How did he get me into the hospital in the first place? Don't concern yourself with these details, he 'arranged' the false diagnosis and there's no doubt about it. I didn't play the game for the rest of the season.

I will add that preceding this false fracture diagnosis Gx1 issued one of his covert signs, 'the greyhound connection'. The sign said that I was soon going to be weighed down on one side (plaster on my left leg, for two months).

At the beginning of August 1969, weeks before the start of the 1969/70 rugby season, I went to Cardiff rugby club to take part in their pre-season training. What do you think Gx1 was doing now? He was of course thinking up new ways to stop my rugby.

At the end of August the Cardiff selectors had a trial game. It was in four ten minute sessions. With players being changed around at the end of each session. I was sent on to the field in the third session, which meant that the selectors were thinking of keeping me on at the club. I felt a bit odd, I could not run, only walk around, I tackled no one and never had the ball once. My feeling a bit odd didn't mean anything to me, I just could not understand it. The selectors did not pick me to stay at the club.

Gx1 had got a hit man to poison me in the hours before the trial. The fact that Gx1 did this is an indication in itself that he had been told I would probably be playing for Cardiff in the coming season. And in his warped mind he had to make sure it did not happen.

Another covert sign was given out by Gx1 in the weeks before this trial game. He actually took part in this one. He pointed something out to me (the PGN number plate), that he knew said, in his covert sign language, that my rugby boots were in a funeral home. My rugby, was 'dead'.

What he meant by my rugby was dead was that top level rugby was, for me, dead. He did not mind me playing the game as long as it was low level rugby (ordinary school rugby and the season I played at Llandaff Tech). But top level rugby was a different matter altogether. In top level rugby influential rugby people could make plans for my rugby. Which would make it a lot more difficult for him to ship me out. Hence he stopped me moving into top level rugby.

Days after the Cardiff trial game I went to Penarth rugby club (just outside Cardiff). In those days they were a top level club. I took part in a trial game they had and was kept on at the club (Gx1 did not poison me prior to this trial game). In the second game of the season I played in their first team, and had a very good game. Gx1 now moved in again. Using his covert activities he dirtied me with the club's selectors, he made sure that I played no more games for the first team. For the rest of the season I played in the second team.

In March 1971 I left my job in Cardiff and started a job in London. For the last couple of months of the rugby season I played for a college where I was studying one day a week. No problems created by Gx1, he didn't mind my playing rugby here.

In June 1971 I moved to a flat in north west London that a friend of mine had bought. He had played for the Llandaff Tech rugby team. It was his idea that we should join pre-season training at a nearby rugby club, which we did in early August. The people at the club, within a week or two, pushed me to the Wasps rugby club which was nearby.

In the first two games of the season I played in the Wasps second team. It is apparent that they wanted me to play in the first team. I say "apparent" because I wasn't told by someone at the club that they wanted me to play in the first team, it is apparent because Gx1 now moved in again with his dirt activities, and there is only one reason for his doing this, it was to stop me playing for the first team.

He immediately arranged to have my car stolen. Presumably he had been told, by someone at the club, that to be selected for the first or second teams a player had to attend the two mid-week evening training sessions. He knew that without the car I couldn't get to the evening training so he arranged for it to be stolen.

I did not connect the car theft to my rugby. I thought it had just happened, by chance, to take place at this time.

The theft caused me to go home to Cardiff for some reason for a weekend, and so I didn't play a game of rugby on that Saturday. The next game I played for the Wasps was a week later, and it was in the third team.

About two weeks after my car was stolen it was found and returned to me. Which meant I got back to mid-week training. So Gx1 still had problems. At this point he got the head of my department at the hospital I worked at to tell me I had to move to accommodation that was near the hospital, to be 'on call'. So I moved out of the flat I was in near the Wasps ground in north west London to the hospital flat, which was in east central London. This meant I did not go to the mid-week evening training sessions. Gx1 had again made sure I did not play for the Wasps first/second teams.

The 'on call' job was rubbish, by that I mean that it was not in the least bit necessary. And I knew this within two weeks of starting it. I stayed in the hospital flat however because my ordinary day job at the hospital was okay, and I ignored the stupid 'on call' bit of it.

Meanwhile I had been moved down to the fourth team at the Wasps. I considered this to be odd because I had played two very good games in the second team. I did not realise that my not going to mid-week training was a reason why I had been dropped. For the rest of the season I was in the fourth team.

Something that's worth knowing is that the top rugby teams in Wales run two teams, a first team and a second team. Whereas in England the top teams run perhaps five or six teams.

For Gx1 this period of fixing things to ensure I did not play for the Wasps first team was a busy time, and he decided to arrange another one of his 'signs' to go with it. This is the 'Diamonds are Forever' sign, the song and film of that name that came out three months after his Wasps 'stop him' activities. The sign meant, in his covert language, that my rugby at the top level (first and second teams at the Wasps) was dead forever.

He connected 'diamonds' to when he got me hit in 1960 in a school baseball game that I was playing in. A baseball game is played on a diamond. The purpose of the hit was to put down, start to destroy, the physical education teacher's 'he is outstanding at rugby' opinion. Now, in 1971, he was 'saying' that when he 'killed' my rugby in 1960 it meant that it was dead forever.

I went to Australia on a one way ticket in June 1972, and stayed at my brother's newly built house. But, contrary to Gx1 plans, I returned to this country three months later in September for the wedding of my ex-rugby mate (I was the best man).

So in September 1972 I was back in Cardiff and took up the job I was in before I moved to London. The job was an electronics technician at a hospital.

Within two or three days of my starting work someone told me that a new rugby team was being created and it would be called Cardiff Hospitals. It seems that it was Mr Q (who was a rugby man) got this team going. He knew that Gx1 had blocked my playing for the Wasps first team and he thought that this new team could push me to Cardiff rugby club, i.e. he wanted to put things right for me on the rugby front.

Gx1 was stunned by my return to this country (I had beaten off his one way ticket). He had the plan to murder my father ready to be put into action some months on from here and I was supposed to be living in Australia when it happened. And here I was back in Cardiff and again being pushed toward Cardiff rugby club. I don't have to tell you what was in his mind. He now came up with new ways to stop me proceeding to top level rugby.

In the department where I worked there was a lad about my age. We first met in 1969 when he started work in the hospital and we had become good friends. Well he said he would join me in playing for the new rugby team. He was in other words going to be my new rugby mate.

Within hours of the start of the first game played by the Cardiff Hospitals team Gx1 had my new rugby mate in a hospital bed with a broken leg. He destroyed my rugby mate in other words. He didn't want anyone helping me to go places in the game. An obvious point comes up here. Why didn't Gx1 get my leg broken? The answer is that he still had ideas on getting me to Australia (one way) and he was going to let me play rugby there (knowing that my brother was a rugby man). So he didn't want to stop my rugby permanently, which is what a broken leg does.

Then in the following week or two Gx1 done a big dirty/smear job on the new rugby team. He told the person who ran the team that we could not use a parks pitch as our home ground. And that we could have a field in the grounds of a mental hospital to use as our home ground (a pitch was soon marked out and posts put up). Can you see the situation that was now in place? Visiting teams told their players to go to a mental hospital to play the game. Some no doubt thought it was a crude joke.

Near the end of the season with Cardiff hospitals Gx1 got a hit man to fire an electron/laser beam into me to stop me going to Cardiff rugby club. The beam hit my upper left leg. It felt like a 240 volt shock.

By the time the start of the next season arrived, the 1973/74 season, the Cardiff Hospitals team had just about folded. It was no more. The idea that Mr Q had, that the team could take me to Cardiff rugby club, had not materialised. I left the hospital job and did not play rugby at all in this 73/74 season.

Mr Q was still unhappy about what had been done to my rugby at the Wasps and he was looking for another way to put things right for me on the rugby front. It was presumably his efforts that got me to apply to start a full time course at Swansea university in September 1974. This was a way to put my rugby right. I left the job I was in and started the full time course.

Mr Q had the following lined up for me. He arranged for a friend of his son to meet me at the college sports ground. We started to go out for a drink together one night a week. He introduced me to the daughter of the secretary of the Welsh Rugby Union, Miss K. She sometimes joined us, usually with a girlfriend, for a drink. The idea Mr Q had was that I could perhaps start a relationship with her, and this would lead to my playing for Swansea rugby club.

Gx1, need I tell you, was aware of what was going on. The plans he had all through the 1960s (murder my father in 1973 at the end of the mortgage, using 'natural causes', ship me out one way to Australia) had taken a severe knock when I, having been 'shipped out' in 1972, returned to this country after only three months in Australia. The result was that he had revised his plans. He carried on with the first part of the 1973 hit of my father but postponed the second part, killing him using poison, until, it seems, he got me on a new one way ticket to Australia.

For Gx1 my starting at Swansea university was a big problem, if things went okay for me it would stop the new 'one way ship out ticket' he had ready for me. He knew that in the ordinary run of things I would play rugby for the university, and that would lead to my playing for Swansea rugby club. So what did he do? As soon as I arrived at the college to start the course he told someone on the college staff to make sure I didn't play for the rugby team. And this was done by dirtying me with one of the lads who ran the rugby team. The result was I was not selected for the first team or even the second team (when it occasionally had a game).

Mr Q was nevertheless proceeding with his plan to get me to Swansea rugby club. My friendship with Miss K was going well. I thought she was a very decent female, and I was willing to start a relationship with her if I had the chance.

My relationship with Miss D was at an end as far as I was concerned. I hadn't actually finished it, for reasons previously stated, but surely it wouldn't be long before she packed me in. You could say I had made a big mistake by asking her out in the first place. Some months before I asked her out I had decided that she was not at all my type. And when I did ask her out I sensed something was up. The "something was up" was Gx1. He used his covert influence to get me going with her knowing that she was trouble and that she suited the 'ship out' plan that he had for me, the new ship out plan (she could be shipped with me when married).

In February 1975 the news got to Gx1 that it looked like me and Miss K would start going together. He did not want this to happen. If I started a relationship with her it would mean I'd stop Miss D. And he did not want me to stop Miss D because he intended to use her to stop my study at the college (which was necessary to keep his plans on track).

This news was forwarded to Miss D's mother and her godfather. They did not like being told that I would soon be finishing with her to start with some other girl in Swansea. Miss D had been pushed on to me in 1973 using the 'innocent church going girl' line and it would be a severe dent to her public image if I 'chucked her in'.

Gx1 decided he was going to stop me starting a relationship with Miss K. And to do it he was going to use more of his dirt activities.

I had a room in a house that was about three quarters of a mile from the college. Easter, the end of March, was approaching. I had no intention of returning to Cardiff for the three week break. Until, that is, I found, in the days before Easter, that I had to vacate my room. This made me return to Cardiff for three weeks.

Gx1 had told the college accommodation office to get me out of the place. He wanted me back in Cardiff for the Easter break, it would mean I would see Miss D, i.e. he could then use the line, 'he has returned to Cardiff to see her, he must like her'.

I will mention here that three months earlier, at Christmas, I had left Swansea at 4pm on Christmas eve to return to my parents house in Cardiff. I could have returned to Cardiff a week earlier, when the lectures finished for the holiday break. This illustrates my lack of interest in Miss D, i.e. I did not go to Cardiff to see her as soon as the holiday break started.

Anyway it's Easter now and it is obvious that Gx1 fed into the college words like, 'he has a wonderful church going girlfriend in Cardiff, he should marry her, stop his study, fail him, it will get him back to Cardiff, and he will marry her'. Why is it obvious? I will tell you.

After Easter I moved into a guest house a half mile from the college, whilst I looked for more suitable, cheaper, accommodation.

I was at the guest house for two weeks. During this time the landlady, who talked a lot at breakfast every day (I was the only guest), said to me, 'you should marry your girlfriend in Cardiff'. I was astonished. She knew almost nothing about her (she had asked me if I had a girlfriend and I said yes, in Cardiff, and that was about all she knew). Her husband was on the staff at the college.

You see what I mean? Gx1 had fed in to the college the Miss D stuff, and it had got fed through to the guest house. The place was used to force me into marrying Miss D. But it didn't come off. So Gx1 thought up another way to stop me and Miss K starting a relationship.

It was now the latter part of April. I hadn't seen Miss K for about two months. I somehow got a message asking me to meet her, and a girlfriend, outside a pub that was adjacent to Swansea rugby club's ground prior to one of their games. The meeting was not my idea. She was giving me a chance to ask her out, start a relationship with her.

At this meeting with Miss K and her girlfriend, Gx1, who was of course up on what was going on, got a hit man, a barman, to put a poison in the drink I bought. The result was that Miss K's interest in me ceased. He had got what he wanted. Now all he had to do was get me stopped at the college.

Weeks later two lecturers gave me forged/altered documents in one of the subjects in the end of academic year examinations (66, Miss D).

I didn't know about the forgery at the time, I thought it was a mistake in the preparation of the exam papers. I was given a fail in the subject (I passed the other subjects). It meant I had to re-sit the exam in September, and I'd have to pass it then to be able to continue at the college.

At the end of June I got a job in Swansea for the summer break, which once again illustrates my lack of interest in Miss D.

In early August I went to Swansea rugby club to take part in their pre-season training. This took place two evenings a week.

The selectors didn't have a trial game and instead when the season started at the beginning of September they went straight into selecting teams for the games. From the training it was obvious to me that I should get a game in the second team. I wasn't thinking about the first team, I just knew I should be in the second team, but for some unknown reason the selectors wouldn't pick me. I recall being at three second team games in which I wasn't selected to play (I was a reserve).

The reason why I wasn't selected for the second team is now obvious of course. Gx1 had told someone at the club to make sure I was not selected for any of their games (second or first team). He knew that very soon I was going to be stopped at the university, and, with no reason to stay in Swansea, I'd return to Cardiff. Which is exactly what he wanted. If I started playing for the second team it would give me a reason for staying in Swansea when my study was stopped (and presumably I'd look for a job there).

Meanwhile at the university students were starting to arrive (from all over the country) ready for the start of the academic year in October. Rugby training had begun and the college had it's first game in mid-

September against a local team. I was selected for this game (the first team).

Where was Gx1 here? Well he knew that he had in effect stopped me at the college three months earlier (the forged documents exam) so he wasn't concerned about what happened to my rugby at the college after that. I'd be given another fail at the re-sit exam and I'd be stopped, out of Swansea university, in September, and back to Cardiff, and that was all that mattered to him.

My being selected for the college first team means that SV (the Gx1 hit man on the college staff who made sure I did not play for the first or second teams when I started at the college a year earlier) was not, at this September time, paying any attention to me, i.e. he had finished the 'stop him' job three months earlier (when he took part in the forged documents activities). So he was not now bothering to block my rugby.

And as for the lad who ran the rugby team who made sure I did not play in the team at the start of the previous season (as arranged by SV), well he was not at the college. Presumably he'd finished his course in June.

In this first game of the season for the college I played on the right wing and scored two tries.

In the third week in September I was told I could not continue at the college because I had failed the re-sit exam (the forged documents subject).

The next day I returned to Cardiff to live at my parents house.

This is where Gx1 got another shock. Within days of my return to Cardiff I went to Cardiff university (UCC) and saw someone about starting with them on a full time course. I was accepted onto a course.

I commenced at the college and went to the rugby team's training. After one game I was in the first team. Gx1, being caught completely unaware by my starting at UCC, had not had time to fix/arrange things with staff at the college to ensure that I never played for the rugby team. So he used another way to stop my rugby. He got a hit man to fire an electron/ laser beam into my chest during this first game that I played for the UCC first team. I went to hospital and was told to stop my rugby for three months. Gx1 had got what he wanted.

My relationship with Miss D had gone on for far too long, she hadn't finished it (which is what I had hoped for) and so I finished it at the beginning of January, knowing that I could be hit for doing so.

And that is exactly what did happen. Gx1 fed into UCC, 'stop his study, it will get him back to an innocent church going girl, he should marry her'.

In the second half of the season I played in the college's first team but Gx1 made sure, using his dirt methods, that my rugby went nowhere.

In June I was given false fail results. I re-sat them in September but I was stopped. Gx1 had again got what he wanted.

The 'Off the Bottom of the Pack' Deals

We have all heard of the phrase 'dealing off the bottom of the pack', with reference to card games. Well I now take you to the hushed hall in a british university in 1975. The hall was used as a venue for an end of academic year examination for about thirty students. I was one of them.

The subject, throughout the academic year, was split into two parts, one lecturer for each part. And there was one three hour examination for each part at the end of the academic year.

In the first of the two examinations, with all the students, including me, sat silently at our single person desks, one of the two lecturers, also known as an invigilator in this situation, walked around giving each student a copy of the question paper. He was the only member of staff in the hall. I noticed nothing untoward in this procedure. But when I looked at the question paper I saw something extraordinary.

I won't go into the details now, you can see them in my earlier books. What I will say here is that the lecturer, who, as an invigilator was supposed to make sure that the examination was conducted in a fair and proper manner, had given me 'one off the bottom of the pack'.

The pack contained the correct question papers for the examination, on the bottom of the pack he had a fixed, altered, question paper that he gave to me. It had the correct heading for the examination, which was "Paper I", but it had the wrong questions in it. The paper had been deliberately altered, it was a forged document (a document intended to deceive and defraud).

I thought that all the students had received the same question paper. And I got on with attempting to answer the questions even though my revision had been done for the proper/correct Paper I questions. I left the examination early and returned to my accommodation.

The altered examination question paper I had been given meant that in the second examination (some days later) I would have to be given a paper that matched it, i.e. I would have to be given another fixed/altered question paper. And the necessary question paper was made by a member of staff.

The second examination arrived. I was sat at a desk in one of the middle columns of four columns of single person desks, about two desks from the back, meaning that I had a good view of what was happening in most of the hall that was in front of me. The lecturer/invigilator, a different person this time, and again he was the only member of staff in the hall, was giving out the question papers. He was at the front of my column of desks and he was proceeding up the column toward me. When he was two or three desks in front of me he paused and gave me a long look, why is he looking at me I thought. When he reached me he gave me a question paper then carried on to the next student who was behind me.

He had given me 'one off the bottom of the pack'. I just accepted the question paper. I was not looking closely at 'the deal', well I was in a college/university examination. Corrupt 'dealing' was unheard of. All I saw was a question paper being placed on my desk. It was the second fixed/altered question paper I had been given in a matter of days.

The lecturer pausing to look at me when he was two/three desks away from me was presumably when he was making sure that he had the fixed question paper, which was located on the bottom of the pack, ready to give to me.

Once again I thought all the students had received the same as me. I had no idea that I'd been the only one to receive a wrong/fixed question paper. I finished the examination and returned to my accommodation.

It was three months later when I realised, for the first time, that some people who were external to the university were out to cause problems for me. Keep me down, stop my university study.

A few years later it became obvious to me that Gx1 was the person who was out to keep me down (he was one of the "some people"). He was in a high level government position. He had used his position to arrange the corrupted examination.

Number 66 Before 1973

Let me take a closer look at the appearance of number 66 in this affair. It was used at the 66 forgery in UCS, it was to 'say' that I was on route for Miss D, she lived at a 66, and that meant it was out of UCS for me, i.e. out of Swansea and back to Cardiff (she lived near Cardiff). There is also the 66 car I bought near the end of my stay in Swansea. And there is the route 66 book when I was at UCC, this time the 66 was to say it was going to be out of UCC and Miss D for me. The intention being to push me back to her, I had finished with her three months earlier (I had found out that she was trouble).

Gx1 used number 66 as a 'sign' that said he was making covert arrangements that were intended to force me into marrying Miss D (and stop me getting a degree). He wanted me married to her because when that happened he could ship me out (with her) and complete the plan to murder my father.

So it looks like, from what I have said so far in the material I have produced on this affair, that Miss D just happened, by chance, to be living at a number 66 and Gx1 decided, in 1975 when I was at UCS, to start using the 66 for his, 'you to Miss D', signs. Yes and that's okay, but there is more to it than that. Miss D, with her parents, did not 'just happen' to be living at a 66. They were moved into the place by Gx1. I will explain.

I start by going to the 1940s 'knife in the trunk'. It would be more accurate to call the knife an indian dagger. It had a curved blade in a sheath, with a bone or ivory handle that had metal fittings at each end of the handle, and a slim chain that ran between the metal fittings. Well in the word dagger there is a 66.

The knife in the trunk was to 'say' that the knife was going into my father in later years. And in the early fifties it went into him when my brother was knifed (knifing my brother was in effect knifing my father). Gx1 arranged to have my brother's nose broken at night when asleep and chloroformed. It was to 'say' that he, my brother, was being knifed. The knifing took the form (as well as the broken nose) of poisoning him before a welsh boys rugby trial to ensure he did not play for the Wales Boys, and getting him out of school before important examinations were to take place to ensure he didn't get the excellent results he was expected to get. Then, some years later, he was 'shipped out' (permanently). In metaphorical terms he had been 'killed' in this country, 'knifed', because he was a very bright son of a worker.

In the warped mind of Gx1 workers were commies. He, being a government policing official, had been directed into this sort of thinking by the people that ran this country. Bear in mind that the Cold War (anti-commies, anti-workers) had been government policy since 1946.

Gx1 had plans to kill my father in 1973 (at the end of the mortgage). And he wanted me out of the way, living in Australia with my brother when the hit took place. He restricted my life right through the fifties, sixties and early seventies to ensure that nothing got in the way of the 'ship out' plan that he had for me.

In 1968/70 Gx1 got the idea given to my brother that a newly built house was the thing to go for (up to this time he and his wife were in a rented flat). Gx1 wanted him to be living in suitable accommodation for when he shipped me there in the early seventies. And my brother bought a plot of land in a large area that was going to have new houses built on it. The plot was number 66.

The plot number was a Gx1 'sign'. He had arranged to have my brother directed to it (using perhaps a 'special offer price'). He was referring to the 1950s when he put the knife into him, the 66 dagger. He was 'saying' that, when he wanted to, he was still running things.

So with 66 first appearing in the 1940s dagger and then making a second appearance in the 1968/70 plot of land it makes it very, very, unlikely that Miss D just happened, by coincidence, to be living in a 66 in 1973 when I started to go out with her. In other words, with Gx1 around, fixing things, it was not a coincidence. He moved her parents into a 66 for his 'sign' purposes.

Gx1 got me to Australia in 1972 on a one way ticket, I was supposed to stop there (find a job and settle there). But somehow, after a stay of only three months I returned to Cardiff. Needless to say Gx1 was very unhappy about this and he immediately formed new plans to get me back there (these included continuing to restrict or stop my rugby).

I took up the hospital job I'd been in before I moved to London. At about this time Miss D (aged sixteen) started work in the department I was in. It seems to me that Gx1 had picked her out (from some sort of covert trouble list that he had, perhaps a list of 'rear sex' females that he could get in on at a later date) as a female who could be shipped out when married to me, and he got her into the job.

And in the months that followed he attached a 'sign' to her that said she was on route for me. And he did this by getting her parents to move to a flat that was number 66. It was a council flat so the move was no problem for him. The 66 'said' that she was on route for me and Australia when we were married.

Then, at the end of the 1972/73 rugby season, Gx1, having again stopped me proceeding to Cardiff rugby club (and a decent female), got her pushed in front of me. Mr E (who was one of his 'yes sir, no sir' people) did the push. But I wasn't in the least bit interested in her, she was in no way suited to me.

I was aged 25, Miss D was 17. The females I had gone out with in earlier years were always about my age. That means, for example, that when I was working in London, aged 23/24, the females I had gone out with were all, what I could call, mature females. Miss D was, by comparison, a non-starter.

Months later Gx1, the knife man, used his covert influence to get me to start a relationship with her. He knew that she was trouble. She suited the new ship out, 'kill', plan that he had for me (it was marry the 66, Miss D, then get shipped to plot 66 land). Recall here, 'killing WT softly with his son', sung by Miss D.

In the next three years Gx1 hit me a number of times in his efforts to get me married to her. I somehow managed to not marry her and I did not get shipped out.

'Yes Sir, No Sir' People

I will say some words here on the willingness of people to do whatever their manager, or an official (such as a policeman) asks them to do. Of course in the usual run of things they say, 'yes, ok'. But some people say 'yes, ok' when the request is clearly out of order.

When someone enters a college on a full time course a contract exists between them. The college receives money from that person (grant, loan) and supplies the person with an education service (lectures etc).

All contracts are based on the proper and honest principles. If activities carried out by either party to the contract are not in line with this then a breach of contract exists.

The staff at Swansea university who participated in the forged documents activities quite obviously breached/broke the basic principles of the contract.

The lecturer who gave me the forged (altered) document in the first examination did so because a member of staff who was senior to him had asked/ told him to do it. Where was his integrity, his natural ability to say, 'I'm not doing that because it is obviously an improper act'? Answer, it was nowhere to be seen.

The "senior" member of staff could have been told what to do by a member of staff who was senior to him, such as the registrar. Where was the integrity of the registrar or the "senior" member of staff? Again it was nowhere to be seen.

Gx1 was the source of the altered document

instructions. He knew it was the criminal acts of making and using forged documents but he would not have fed these words into the college because it would stop them going ahead with his instructions. And evidently none of the staff realised it was forgery. They thought it was just altering an important document and then presenting it as the genuine document.

Then there was the dirtying me, getting me blacked, with one of the lads that ran the rugby team, to ensure I did not play for the college. Presumably this was done by SV (on Gx1 instructions). Again this had to be a breach of contract by a member of staff. What he did was in no way "proper and honest" as required by the contract. Where was his integrity?

The college had a contract with me, not with Gx1. Their staff should have adhered to the basic principles of the contract and told Gx1, with his odd instructions, to 'get lost'.

A year later Gx1 had to use a different procedure at Cardiff university. The staff there would not accept his instructions (to stop me) and so he fed false information into the college, to deceive/trick them into doing what he wanted.

Also under this chapter heading are the people who said, 'yes sir, no sir', to what Gx1 asked/told them to do and then put poison in my food or drink.

And then there are the people who did various other vile/criminal acts, because Gx1 had asked/told them to do it.

Laser, Electron and Sound Beam Devices

In October 1980 I had a thirty second block covertly done to my natural thinking when I was expected to say something at a seated public meeting in a large hall. A government hit man covertly fired a device at my head that created a loud continuous high frequency noise in my hearing, it was kept on for thirty seconds. This stunned me and made me incapable of doing anything (speaking or hearing anything else) for the duration of the sound.

It was done, as I've told you earlier, to plant false evidence into my dispute with UCC (to ensure I lost the support of UCC).

I had stood up to reply to the chairman who had asked me for more details on a question I had put to the panel that were seated on the stage. Before I said a word I was hit. It stunned me and I collapsed on to the seat I was next to. At the end of the thirty seconds, when the noise stopped, my normal senses returned to me.

How could I have heard this very loud sound that lasted for thirty seconds when all the other people in the hall had not heard it? It did not make sense to me in 1980. But by 1994 I had got more information together and decided that high frequency audio sound waves had been aimed at my head (my ears) by someone in the seats behind me using a device that somehow kept the high frequency audio sound within a beam. Hence only I heard it.

The loud continuous high frequency noise was an

audio tone of about 3 khz (on the internet I have listened to audio tones and picked on the 3khz tone as being a close match to what I experienced in 1980).

In 2022 I got more information on directional audio sound (the device that was used to hit me at the town hall meeting used this technique). On sale today to the public are speakers that can direct audio sound into a small area. I don't know when they first appeared on the market but it could be around ten years ago. They are sometimes used in museums and art galleries.

The speakers are used to direct audio sound to people who are stood in a small area in front of an exhibit. The audio contains a voice recording that gives details on the exhibit. When the recording ends it starts again.

The speaker could be fixed to the ceiling (or hung from the ceiling) and it directs its sound beam downward to the area in front of the exhibit. When the person in front of the exhibit moves out of the area (to the next exhibit) he leaves the voice recording sound beam and enters the quiet zone of the museum/gallery.

I will give you a few technical details on how a directional audio sound beam is generated. The word ultrasound is used to define sound frequencies that are above the human audio range. These ultrasound frequencies are obtained from a crystal/material that physically vibrates when a voltage is applied to it. This vibration is the ultrasound.

One characteristic ultrasound has is that it can be channelled into a narrow beam (like a beam from a torch).

Aim the ultrasound speaker's beam from it's location on the ceiling to the floor in front of an exhibit and you have a confined area full of ultrasound. The audio recording is then mixed into the source of the ultrasound beam and this produces a modulated ultrasound beam. The result is that a person stood in the ultrasound beam in front of the exhibit can hear the audio recording (but not the ultrasound carrier frequency).

At the town hall the government hit man who aimed the directional audio sound device at my head was, as I have said, in one of the seats behind me. He aimed the device upward from his lap at my head, perhaps at 45 degrees from the horizontal. The beam continued upward after my head to the hall's ceiling where it ceased.

No one else in the hall heard the loud thirty second 3khz audio tone because they were kept out of the beam.

In earlier years Gx1 hit men, on two separate occasions, covertly fired laser/electron beams at me. One of these gave me a jolt that felt like a 240 volt wire had touched my leg (the Gx1 intention behind the hit was to stop me going to, playing for, Cardiff RFC). The second felt like a 200 volt wire had touched my chest (the Gx1 intention here was to stop my rugby for three months).

The devices I have talked about in the last paragraph, devices for firing at, incapacitating, a person, can only be obtained by government employees. The british government, and the governments of other countries, do not talk about them in public, they are hidden away in their covert departments. The reason why governments say nothing about these devices is of course that they don't want the public to start using them. If a conventional bullet hits a man everyone knows that someone fired a gun at him. If a laser or electron beam hits a man all he knows is that he had a severe pain for some unknown reason (e.g. 240 volt jolt). And no one, apart from the person who fired the device, knows why he was incapacitated for some seconds. Turn up the power and laser/electron beam devices could be used to kill a person. The death probably gets diagnosed as a heart attack. Hence the killer gets away with it.

So it is not surprising that governments don't want the public to use these devices. But to try to pretend that laser, and electron beam devices that are used to incapacitate people don't exist is I think an un-realistic and naive way of going about things. Well it is generally known that lasers and electron beams are widely used for industrial and medical purposes.

The proper way to deal with the situation is I think for governments to accept that laser/electron beam devices that can be used for incapacitating people exist and to make it illegal for a member of the public to use one. And it follows that it would be illegal to sell the devices to the public, and to manufacture the devices without government permission.

9 781738 503889